# SMOKE & OAK

## The Shared Legacy of Bourbon and Cigars

*An American Story of Craft, Culture & the Science of a Perfect Pairing*

Sebastian Saviano

THE AMERICAN CIGAR PRESS

**Smoke & Oak**
*The Shared Legacy of Bourbon and Cigars*

Published by
The American Cigar Press
An imprint of Deriva Publishing

ISBN 979-8-998-51170-7 (hardcover)
ISBN 979-8-9985117-6-9 (paperback)
ISBN 979-8-9992336-0-8 (ebook)

LCCN: 2025936408

First printing, April 2025
Second printing, with corrections, May 2026

For inquiries or permissions, visit www.DerivaPublishing.com

Printed in the United States of America and in other countries.

This book is a work of historical research. While every effort has been made to ensure accuracy, the author and publisher assume no responsibility for errors, omissions, or any consequences arising from its use.

*The American Cigar Series*
Volume 2 of a four-volume nonfiction series exploring the cultural, political, and sensory history of cigars in American life:

Vol. 1 — *America's Cigar Story*
Vol. 2 — *Smoke & Oak*
Vol. 3 — *The American Puro*
Vol. 4 — *Cigar America*

*For those who slow down, light up, and pour with purpose—*
*may you always find good company in the burn and the barrel.*

Uncle Sam Approved.

# PREFACE

Pairing bourbon and cigars is more than a pastime. It's a ritual, a conversation between fire and oak, leaf and grain. It's an experience that rewards patience, curiosity, and a well-trained palate. But above all, it's about connection: to tradition, to craft, and to the moment itself.

This book was born not just from personal passion, but from the realization that these pairings carry stories: stories of migration and memory, of labor and landscape, of chemistry and community. Bourbon tells the tale of America's spirit, distilled through fire and time. Cigars, no less storied, speak in leaf and ash of a craft passed down through generations. Together, they offer a dialogue of flavor and feeling that goes far beyond the glass or the draw.

*Smoke & Oak* was written to bring that dialogue into focus. It is part cultural history, part tasting manual, part sensory guide. It explores the roots of bourbon and cigars, the science behind their profiles, and the strategies that make pairings truly sing. Whether you're a seasoned aficionado or a curious newcomer, this book aims to deepen your understanding, and heighten your enjoyment, of two of life's most enduring indulgences.

This is not a rulebook. It's a companion. The goal is not to dictate the perfect pairing, but to inspire discovery. To encourage experimentation. To offer frameworks and flavors that lead you to pairings that feel as personal as they are profound.

Along the way, we honor the hands behind the craft: the farmers, fermenters, blenders, coopers, rollers, and distillers who make this world possible. Their work is not only technical—it is cultural, creative, and steeped in tradition.

So light up. Pour slowly. And enjoy the journey ahead. There's a world of smoke and oak waiting—one pairing at a time.

Sebastian Saviano

# Table of Contents

# Why Bourbon and Cigars

**B**ourbon and cigars have long been paired, not by accident but by shared sensibility. This pairing isn't just about flavor; it's about heritage, ritual, and the slow appreciation of craft. Together, cigars and bourbon evoke a uniquely American story, one rooted in region, resilience, and refinement.

## Shared Heritage

*Both bourbon and cigars have deep American roots, with strong ties to Southern culture, craftsmanship, and tradition.*

Few pairings speak to American tradition as clearly as cigars and bourbon. Both are born of the land, shaped by craftsmanship, and steeped in cultural identity, especially in the American South. Bourbon, legally recognized as a distinctive product of the United States, and cigars, rooted in the South's tobacco legacy and shaped by immigrant labor, have followed parallel paths of pride, resilience, and revival.

Their union conjures the image of leather chairs and oak-paneled rooms, of post-dinner rituals and long conversations. From speakeasies and Southern porches to cigar lounges and distillery tours, this pairing has been a staple in settings where time slows and craft matters.

## Flavor Compatibility

*The charred oak barrels used in bourbon aging often echo the toasted or spicy notes found in cigars.*

Bourbon and cigars don't just share a cultural backdrop—they meet beautifully on the palate. Bourbon's classic profile—notes of vanilla, caramel, oak, spice, and smoke—mirrors and enhances the richness of many cigars:

- **Maduro-wrapped cigars**, with their deep earthiness, cocoa, and leather tones, pair effortlessly with bold, high-proof bourbons. The charred oak barrels used in bourbon aging mirror the toasted and spicy flavors often found in these darker cigars.
- **Connecticut Broadleaf cigars**, known for their sweet, robust character, find natural harmony with bourbons that lean into caramel and brown sugar profiles.

The interplay between smoke and spirit is sensual and layered. It isn't about overpowering the palate. It's about the push and pull between sweet and spice, fire and smoothness, wood and earth.

## A Cultural Pairing Ritual

*Bourbon is sipped, not shot. And so is a fine cigar: slowly, deliberately, with intention.*

Cigars and bourbon share a rhythm. Neither is meant for haste. Both are consumed slowly, intentionally, meant to be savored, not rushed. A premium cigar, like a well-aged bourbon, reveals itself in stages. Each draw or sip brings a new layer, a shift in perception, a conversation starter.

There's also a shared culture of connoisseurship—an appreciation for nuance, process, and provenance. Enthusiasts of both tend to value origin, age, blend, barrel, soil, and story. They speak in tasting notes and vintage years, in wrappers and mash bills. They gather at lounges and tastings, distilleries and cigar bars, often at events where both products are celebrated together.

In recent decades, this connection has only deepened, with cigar lounges stocking curated bourbon selections and distilleries offering cigars during VIP tastings. It's more than cross-marketing. It's cultural resonance.

In short, bourbon and cigars aren't just complementary—they're companions. They come from the same slow world of craft, of heritage passed down in barrels and bales, of indulgence shaped by intention. To understand one is to appreciate the other more fully. And in pairing them, we don't just enjoy a drink or a smoke. We connect to something deeper, older, and undeniably American

## Featured Inside

*Ritual isn't just repetition —*
*it's memory you can taste.*
— From *Smoke & Oak*

# INTRODUCTION

# Smoke & Oak: An American Legacy

Bourbon and cigars share a remarkable legacy, intertwined by craftsmanship, resilience, and a uniquely American cultural heritage. They embody a history marked by tradition, innovation, and sensory richness. This book, *Smoke & Oak*, is an invitation to discover why bourbon and cigars have become so profoundly interconnected, blending historical narratives and scientific insights to deepen our appreciation of these timeless pleasures.

At its heart, *Smoke & Oak* bridges the worlds of history, culture, and sensory science, charting how bourbon and cigars evolved from humble colonial commodities into internationally acclaimed symbols of sophistication. Their parallel paths reveal striking similarities: both faced dramatic disruptions, from Prohibition's devastating impact on bourbon production to the Cuban Embargo's reshaping of the cigar industry. Yet through adversity, these products endured, continually adapting and emerging stronger, transforming setbacks into opportunities for refinement and reinvention.

Part I of this book explores the rich cultural history behind bourbon and cigars, illuminating how each industry developed within distinct regions that shaped their identities and flavor profiles. From the limestone-rich waters of Kentucky to the tobacco fields of Virginia, Connecticut, and Pennsylvania, to the volcanic soils of Nicaragua, we uncover how geography (*terroir*[1]) has been essential in crafting the distinctive character of each. This historical journey provides readers with a vivid narrative of innovation and resilience, tracing their transformation from colonial luxuries to icons of refinement in the modern age.

Yet history alone cannot fully explain the powerful synergy between bourbon and cigars. Part II takes readers beyond the surface, exploring the science of taste and aroma. Here we delve into the molecular interactions of phenolic compounds, terpenes, and esters: the chemical elements that dictate how flavors harmonize or contrast. Understanding these principles enhances not only our appreciation of bourbon and cigars individually but also why their pairing creates uniquely compelling sensory experiences.

Designed for enthusiasts, scholars, professionals, and newcomers alike, this book serves as a comprehensive guide that merges theory with practical advice. It provides tools to refine your palate, deepen your understanding, and cultivate your ability to create memorable pairings. By offering clear, approachable explanations alongside practical guidelines, *Smoke & Oak* gives readers the tools to craft their own bourbon-and-cigar pairings.

Ultimately, *Smoke & Oak* celebrates more than the pairing of bourbon and cigars. It honors the artisans, farmers, distillers, and enthusiasts who shaped these traditions, preserving their heritage while embracing innovation. As you read, you will not only learn why bourbon and cigars complement each other so beautifully but will also experience their enduring appeal firsthand, discovering for yourself why these two crafts remain cherished symbols of American culture.

---

[1]**Terroir:** A French term referring to the environmental factors—such as soil, climate, and topography—that influence the character and flavor of agricultural products. Originally used in wine, it now applies to products like tobacco and bourbon, where place shapes profile.

With this foundation established, we now turn to the beginning of the story: Chapter 1, Origins of an American Pairing (1600s–1800s). It traces the deep roots of both bourbon and cigars in colonial America, weaving together economic development, regional agriculture, cultural symbolism, and political transformation. Here we uncover how two seemingly disparate products, tobacco and whiskey, emerged not only as vital commodities but as twin expressions of early American ingenuity, labor, and identity. The legacies we savor today were forged in these formative centuries.

# PART I

## CHAPTER 1

# Origins of an American Pairing
# (1600s–1800s)

The intertwined history of bourbon and tobacco is not merely a cultural artifact but a rich, complex narrative that stretches back to the earliest days of European settlement in North America. Long before cigars and bourbon became symbols of refinement and luxury, tobacco and distilled spirits were essential economic lifelines that shaped regional development, social customs, and even the foundational politics of the new world. Their shared trajectory goes beyond the convergence of two distinct crafts; it embodies the adaptive spirit of America itself.

This chapter traces how bourbon and cigars emerged from necessity and invention, born from agricultural innovation, driven by economic imperatives, and shaped by cultural exchange. From the colonial period through the post-Revolutionary era, we explore how these goods evolved into enduring symbols of American identity, setting the stage for their later rise as cultural icons.

## Before the Boom: The Roots of an American Pairing

The rise of tobacco and distilled spirits in early America was the result of a unique convergence of indigenous knowledge, European demand, and colonial adaptation. Long before European settlers arrived, Native American cultures had already cultivated and used tobacco for ceremonies, medicine, and trade. Its spiritual and communal importance transcended mere consumption, serving as a medium for communication and ritual across tribes.

Meanwhile, Europeans were aggressively expanding their global trade networks, driven by mercantile ambitions that sought valuable commodities to fuel their economies. The Spanish, English, and French, in their rush to establish colonies in the New World, recognized the commercial potential of crops like tobacco, which had already captured the imagination of Europe's aristocratic and mercantile classes. Introduced by Spanish explorers to Europe in the 16th century, tobacco quickly gained popularity, becoming a high-value commodity almost overnight.

As European colonists established their foothold in the New World, they quickly adapted their agricultural practices to new environments. Nowhere was this adaptation more pronounced than in Virginia, where the fertile soil and humid climate proved ideal for tobacco cultivation. The economic viability of the struggling Jamestown colony was largely rescued by a single, transformative innovation: in 1612, John Rolfe introduced a new, sweeter tobacco strain, marking a foundational moment in American agriculture. Rolfe's new strain boosted Virginia's exports, setting the stage for the colony's commercial transformation. His efforts transformed tobacco from a modest crop into Virginia's most valuable export, laying the foundation for the colony's economic success and shaping its social hierarchy.

As tobacco established itself as a dominant economic force in the South, other regions of colonial America began developing parallel agricultural economies. In the mid-Atlantic and frontier regions, where grain crops such as rye, corn, and barley thrived, settlers turned to a different form of agricultural transformation. Beginning in the early 1700s, Scottish and Irish immigrants in Pennsylvania and Maryland introduced and refined Old World distillation techniques. Drawing on traditions perfected in Scotland, and Ireland, they began applying distillation to local grains. Whiskey at this stage was not a luxury but a practical beverage, safer than often-contaminated water and an efficient way to preserve surplus grain. In these early colonial settlements, whiskey, like tobacco, became both a product of necessity and a symbol of regional identity.

The intersection of these two industries in the colonial era was not merely economic but also cultural. Tobacco and whiskey quickly established themselves as staples of social life. In taverns and homes alike, the act of smoking a pipe or sharing a dram of whiskey became rituals of camaraderie, negotiation, and even political discourse. They conveyed status and identity, serving as markers of hospitality and sophistication.

As colonial settlements expanded and matured, the infrastructure necessary to sustain large-scale tobacco cultivation and whiskey production began to take shape. Tobacco warehouses, distilleries, and merchant trading houses dotted the landscape, transforming previously isolated settlements into bustling economic hubs. Tobacco and whiskey quickly became the lifeblood of an emerging commercial economy that would soon seek independence from its European overlords.

The rise of these industries was emblematic of a broader pattern of adaptation and innovation that defined the early American experience. Tobacco and whiskey, first born of necessity and pragmatism, gradually acquired cultural meaning that transcended mere commerce. They became symbols of resilience, ingenuity, and the uniquely American ability to turn scarcity into abundance.

The roots of this cultural pairing were firmly planted in the colonial era, but their growth would accelerate rapidly as the young nation sought to establish its identity. In the decades that followed, the synergy between tobacco and whiskey would deepen, transforming from mere economic commodities into cultural icons that represented the very spirit of America. As their prominence grew, so too did their influence over the social, political, and economic landscape of the burgeoning nation.

## III.    Foundation of Colonial Commerce

The rapid expansion of tobacco and whiskey production in early America was part of a broader transformation that established these products as cornerstones of colonial commerce. As the colonies matured, so too did their commercial networks, which increasingly revolved around the cultivation of tobacco and the distillation of whiskey.

### Economic Development

The early American economy was driven by the exploitation of natural resources and the establishment of agricultural enterprises capable of producing high-value commodities. Tobacco and whiskey, as agricultural exports, became the most lucrative products in the colonial economy, providing a crucial economic foundation that would support generations of development.

*The Tobacco Boom*

John Rolfe's tobacco breakthrough set in motion a profound economic transformation in Virginia, a shift that would shape colonial agriculture, commerce, and labor systems for generations (see Section II, *Origins: The Pivotal Role of Tobacco in Colonial Development*).

Tobacco production involved more than planting and harvesting. In the 1670s, planters began formalizing systematic curing and grading processes, ensuring consistent tobacco quality for international markets, which was essential for marketing their crops internationally. These advancements allowed American-grown tobacco to compete effectively in European markets, creating an economic model that would dominate colonial exports for centuries.

Yet this success was not without consequences. The intensive cultivation of tobacco required vast amounts of land, prompting constant territorial expansion and contributing to conflicts with Native American populations. Additionally, tobacco's labor-intensive nature made it one of the principal drivers of the transatlantic slave trade, as wealthy planters increasingly relied on enslaved labor to maximize their profits.

## The Rise of Whiskey Distillation

As tobacco drove the southern colonies' economy, whiskey distillation emerged prominently in Pennsylvania and Kentucky, adapting European techniques to New World grains and laying the foundation for uniquely American spirits such as rye and bourbon.

By the late 18th century, Kentucky had quickly established itself as a prime region for whiskey production, with settlers already crafting corn-based spirits that would evolve into bourbon.

Distillation became an economic activity not only for formal businesses but also for small-scale farmers seeking to convert excess grain into a durable, transportable, and highly marketable product. As distillers refined their techniques and developed local reputations, the foundations of a burgeoning whiskey industry began to take shape.

## Economic Infrastructure and Trade Networks

The wealth generated by tobacco and whiskey production did more than enrich individual planters and distillers. It fueled the development of transportation networks, market towns, and financial institutions essential to a growing economy.

In Virginia, tobacco was often shipped directly from plantation wharves to European markets, bypassing traditional urban trade centers. This system of direct exportation enabled planters to amass great wealth and political power. By contrast, whiskey production was more decentralized, with small-scale operations scattered across the frontier. Yet the development of local taverns and trading posts created a network of commerce that connected rural distillers to regional markets.

As the colonies expanded, roads, rivers, and later canals would be developed to facilitate the transportation of tobacco and whiskey. These infrastructural improvements were driven largely by the economic importance of these commodities, underscoring their centrality to early American commercial life.

## Status and Symbolism

The transformation of tobacco and whiskey from mere agricultural products into cultural symbols was as significant as their economic impact. Their commercial success translated directly into social power, as the consumption of tobacco and whiskey became closely associated with status, sophistication, and refinement.

### *The Emergence of Tobacco as a Status Symbol*

In the $17^{th}$ and $18^{th}$ centuries, tobacco had firmly established itself as a luxury commodity in European markets, and its cultivation in America only enhanced this reputation. The growing demand for high-quality tobacco prompted American planters to develop sophisticated methods of grading and branding their products. Tobacco consumption was not only widespread but deeply ritualized, with different forms of smoking signifying distinct social statuses. Wealthier individuals often smoked refined, elegantly crafted clay pipes or early cigars as expressions of sophistication, while laborers and common settlers more frequently used simple clay or wooden pipes for communal smoking. Thus, tobacco became a social display, an integral part of gatherings, negotiations, and daily rituals that communicated one's identity, class, and cultural belonging.

*Whiskey's Social Identity*

While tobacco initially enjoyed a more elevated status, whiskey rapidly gained ground as an essential part of American culture. Its practicality as a commodity and its symbolic value as a drink of the common man made it immensely popular. Unlike tobacco, which was heavily marketed to Europe, whiskey found its primary audience within the colonies themselves.

Taverns elevated whiskey's cultural prominence, as multifunctional social hubs (detailed in Section VII, *Taverns and the Bourbon Economy*). Business transactions, political debates, and even court sessions were often conducted over glasses of whiskey. As Americans began to assert their independence, whiskey became a powerful symbol of local identity and self-sufficiency.

*Tobacco and Whiskey as Markers of Cultural Capital*

By the late 18$^{th}$ century, the pairing of tobacco and whiskey had already begun to emerge as a distinct aspect of American culture. While the act of smoking a pipe or drinking whiskey could be a personal pleasure, it was also a social signal, a statement of identity, taste, and cultural alignment. Whether enjoyed in the drawing rooms of wealthy planters or the rough-hewn taverns of the frontier, tobacco and whiskey were intertwined with the social fabric of early American life.

As colonial America evolved from a patchwork of agricultural settlements into a complex economic and cultural system, tobacco and whiskey would remain at the heart of its development. They were not merely commodities; they functioned as cultural artifacts: ritual goods, instruments of social signaling, and channels of negotiation.

# II. Origins: Tobacco's Role in Colonial Development

Before exploring the broader economic and cultural infrastructure that developed around these commodities, we must return to the pivotal moment that sparked it all: John Rolfe's tobacco breakthrough in 1612.

## Tobacco's Commercial Breakthrough

The year 1612 marks a critical juncture in the history of American tobacco cultivation. It was in this year that John Rolfe, an English settler in the struggling Virginia Colony, made a breakthrough that would alter the colony's fortunes and ultimately shape the economy of the New World.

John Rolfe's success was rooted in his decision to cultivate a milder, sweeter strain of tobacco—*Nicotiana tabacum*—imported from the Caribbean. Unlike the harsher native varieties, this strain was far more appealing to European tastes, which had already developed a craving for tobacco thanks to earlier imports from the Spanish colonies.

Rolfe's innovation sparked an economic revolution: by 1624, Virginia was exporting over 200,000 pounds of tobacco annually. Just six years later, by 1630, exports had soared past 1.5 million pounds, and by 1670, they exceeded 10 million pounds. What had been a struggling settlement was now an export-driven economy, with tobacco firmly established as the colony's primary economic engine and cultural backbone.

The commercial breakthrough of tobacco transformed Virginia's agricultural landscape. Planters quickly began to expand their operations, investing in land and labor to increase their output. This rapid growth was facilitated by the adoption of systematic curing and grading techniques, which ensured consistency in quality and established a standard of excellence that would dominate the transatlantic trade.

Tobacco cultivation was no longer an experiment. It was a sophisticated agricultural industry. By the 1670s, tobacco had become Virginia's most valuable export, with production rapidly expanding into Maryland and North Carolina. This transformation had far-reaching implications for the economy, society, and culture of the colonies.

## Transformation of Agriculture and Trade

The dramatic success of tobacco as a cash crop sparked a broader transformation in colonial agriculture and trade. As demand grew in

European markets, colonial planters refined their techniques and expanded their operations to meet the insatiable appetite for American tobacco. The principles that emerged during this period—standardization, specialization, and market-driven production—would later influence the burgeoning whiskey industry as well.

The economic impact of tobacco extended beyond mere profit. It shaped the labor force, with the increasing reliance on indentured servants and, eventually, enslaved Africans to meet the demands of large-scale production. The institution of slavery became intertwined with the cultivation of tobacco, creating a deeply entrenched economic model that would persist for centuries.

This era also witnessed the development of elaborate trade networks connecting the American colonies to England and beyond. Ports like Jamestown and Williamsburg in Virginia grew into bustling centers of commerce, where merchants brokered deals and established partnerships that would form the backbone of the colonial economy.

The transformative power of tobacco's commercial breakthrough also reshaped colonial society. The rapid expansion of agriculture prompted debates over land use, labor rights, and the distribution of wealth. It accelerated the formation of social hierarchies, with successful planters acquiring land and wealth that allowed them to dominate local politics and cultural life.

The agricultural revolution sparked by John Rolfe's innovation in 1612 established key economic patterns—standardization, specialization, and market-oriented production—that would soon be applied to other frontier industries. As settlers moved westward into grain-rich regions, they brought these principles with them, laying the foundation for another defining American tradition: whiskey distillation. In the next section, we explore how the lessons of tobacco cultivation helped shape the rise of a distinctly American spirit.

# III. The Birth of Luxury Trade

By the late 17<sup>th</sup> century, the refinement of tobacco and whiskey marked the beginning of their cultural ascent, transforming them from mere commodities into luxury goods that would shape American society for centuries.

**Tobacco & Whiskey as Early American Icons**

As tobacco became a reliable cash crop, its consumption moved from mere indulgence to a marker of social status. European elites prized fine tobacco for its refined aroma and smooth flavor, making it a centerpiece of high society. The emergence of cigar culture followed, with wealthy gentlemen often pairing their indulgence with the era's finest spirits.

At the same time, whiskey was beginning to carve out its own identity. Although its production was still largely an informal, household practice, the drink's popularity continued to grow. Its appeal lay in its accessibility. Grains were more abundant than tobacco, making whiskey a more democratic indulgence. But even as it became widespread, the spirit retained an air of craftsmanship and heritage, particularly when prepared by experienced distillers who had perfected their methods over generations.

The symbolic power of tobacco and whiskey was not lost on the American colonists themselves. Plantation owners, merchants, and political leaders increasingly embraced these products as representations of cultural sophistication. Taverns, which played a central role in the social life of the colonies, became hubs where these luxuries were consumed and celebrated. A well-aged spirit and a finely rolled cigar became declarations of taste, power, and refinement.

Their cultural significance grew alongside their economic rise. As symbols of prosperity and status, these commodities became integral to social rituals. Sharing a cigar or offering a guest a glass of well-aged whiskey were gestures that went beyond hospitality; they were affirmations of social standing and sophistication.

## Fusion of European Craftsmanship and Indigenous Knowledge

The transformation of tobacco and whiskey into luxury goods was not solely the product of European ingenuity. Rather, it was the fusion of European craftsmanship and Indigenous knowledge that made these products so exceptional.

Tobacco cultivation, as practiced by Native Americans, had deep cultural and medicinal significance. Indigenous communities had long understood the plant's properties, using it for religious ceremonies, healing rituals, and social interactions. Their techniques for cultivating and curing tobacco were instrumental in shaping the methods later adopted by European settlers.

What European colonists brought to the table was a commercial mentality focused on standardization, refinement, and large-scale production. The marriage of these two traditions created a product that was not only popular but commercially viable on a massive scale. The curing, fermenting, and grading methods that developed during the late 1600s reflected both indigenous wisdom and European commercial pragmatism.

Meanwhile, whiskey's evolution followed a similar pattern. Scots-Irish immigrants brought their distillation knowledge to the New World, applying their techniques to the abundant grains available in the colonies. What began as small-batch, home-distilled spirits gradually evolved into a more standardized production process, particularly as settlers moved westward and began exploiting new resources.

The cultural exchange that defined this period was not without its conflicts and inequalities. The exploitation of enslaved labor, particularly in the tobacco fields, underscores the darker side of this economic boom. Nevertheless, the blending of indigenous practices with European craftsmanship created products that would become central to the cultural identity of the American colonies.

## Indigenous Roots Beneath the Barrel

Though Native American communities did not practice distillation in the European sense, their agricultural legacy deeply shaped the foundations of American whiskey. The most significant contribution? Corn.

Long before settlers arrived, Indigenous peoples cultivated maize as a staple crop, mastering its growth across varied climates. When Scots-Irish immigrants brought distillation techniques to the New World, they adapted their recipes, substituting Old World barley with New World corn. This pivotal shift gave birth to a uniquely American spirit: bourbon.

Indigenous knowledge also informed settler understandings of the land: its seasons, water sources, and crop cycles. While often overlooked, these foundational contributions made the frontier's whiskey revolution possible. Without the corn, there would be no bourbon.

Innovation and refinement were continual, evolving with each generation of producers. As European techniques adapted to the materials and conditions of the New World, entirely new products emerged. Bourbon, for example, was not just a replication of Scotch or Irish whiskey; it was a uniquely American spirit born from the fertile cornfields and limestone-filtered water of Kentucky. Likewise, American-grown tobacco—particularly the varieties cultivated in Virginia and Maryland—acquired a flavor and quality distinct from its Caribbean and South American counterparts.

By the early 1700s, the colonies had established themselves as producers of premium tobacco and whiskey. Their popularity in European markets reinforced their cultural status at home, where they were celebrated as symbols of wealth, craftsmanship, and regional pride. As the 18th century approached, both industries would continue to evolve, refined through experimentation and adaptation.

## IV. Tobacco & Whiskey: America's First Luxury Pairing

By the early 1700s, tobacco had firmly established itself as a luxury good, cementing its role through the emergence of tobacco houses. These fashionable meeting places became essential hubs for merchants, planters, and political elites, where tobacco was not merely consumed but ritualized as a marker of refinement and status. While pipe smoking remained the dominant form of tobacco consumption among both the wealthy and working classes, cigars were beginning to make their way into elite circles by the mid-1700s, though they were still largely imported rather than domestically produced. The act of sharing a cigar or a pipe became a gesture of camaraderie, friendship, and social standing, often accompanied by fine spirits to elevate the sensory experience.

Tobacco's economic power during this period was profound. As a high-value cash crop, it generated immense wealth for plantation owners, traders, and merchants alike. The economic success of tobacco drove agricultural innovation, advances in shipping logistics, and the development of competitive branding practices as planters sought to establish their products as symbols of quality and prestige. In this context, tobacco was more than a commodity. It was a cultural artifact, deeply entwined with social rituals and economic ambition, shaping both private lives and public identities.

As tobacco cemented its place among the colonies' elite circles, whiskey was quietly undergoing its own transformation, from humble frontier necessity to a symbol of skilled craftsmanship and regional pride.

*Whiskey as a Symbol of American Craftsmanship*

Tobacco and whiskey fueled colonial commerce through distinct economic pathways. Tobacco was a global export, shipped in vast quantities across the Atlantic and driving the wealth of Southern planters and port cities. Whiskey, by contrast, circulated primarily within the colonies. It connected rural distillers to regional markets and became a staple of frontier economies, where it functioned as both a trade good and a form of currency.

Despite their divergent trade routes, both industries underpinned local economies, sustained merchant activity, and drove infrastructure development, from plantation ports to frontier trading posts. More than just commodities, tobacco and whiskey helped weave a commercial fabric that linked disparate colonial regions, creating interdependencies that would underpin the early American economy.

## Regional Influence

While tobacco and whiskey both emerged as luxury goods, their cultural and economic significance varied greatly by region. These regional distinctions would come to define the unique character of American tobacco and whiskey, setting the stage for their evolution into symbols of American craftsmanship and heritage.

### Tobacco's Regional Dominance

Tobacco cultivation flourished particularly in Virginia, Maryland, and parts of North Carolina. Each region developed its own distinct approach to tobacco farming, influenced by local geography, climate, and labor practices:

- **Virginia's Brightleaf Tobacco**: Virginia became synonymous with the production of high-quality brightleaf tobacco, prized for its mild flavor and smooth smoke. The plantations of the Tidewater region, with their rich, fertile soils, produced leaves that commanded high prices in both domestic and international markets.
- **Maryland's Sweet Tobacco**: Maryland planters developed a strain known for its sweetness and aromatic qualities. This variety, while less popular abroad, gained a loyal following among American consumers.
- **North Carolina's Dark-Fired Tobacco**: Dark-fired tobacco, a heartier

and more robust leaf, was cultivated in parts of North Carolina and Kentucky. It was particularly suited for cigars and pipe tobacco, establishing a niche market that would continue to expand over the centuries.

*Whiskey's Regional Variations*

Whiskey production was more evenly distributed across the colonies but was particularly prominent in the mid-Atlantic and southern regions. Each area developed its own unique approach to distillation, resulting in the emergence of distinct styles:

- **Pennsylvania Rye Whiskey**: The Scots-Irish settlers of Pennsylvania brought with them a tradition of rye whiskey distillation, producing a spicy, robust spirit that would become a local favorite.
- **Maryland's Milder Rye**: While similar to Pennsylvania's, Maryland's rye version was often distilled to be smoother and less harsh, appealing to a broader audience.
- **Corn Whiskey and Bourbon in Kentucky**: In the 1780s and 1790s, settlers in Kentucky began refining corn-based whiskey, laying the groundwork for bourbon whiskey. The state's limestone-filtered water, fertile soil, and favorable climate created ideal conditions for producing what would become known as bourbon whiskey.
- **Southern Distilleries**: Early whiskey production in Virginia and Tennessee helped establish core practices—like corn-based distillation, local trade, and barrel aging—that laid the cultural and technical foundation for what would later emerge as Kentucky bourbon and Tennessee whiskey.

Tennessee whiskey and Kentucky bourbon follow nearly identical production standards: at least 51% corn in the mash, aging in new charred oak barrels, and strict federal regulation. Legally, Tennessee whiskey qualifies as bourbon, but one key difference sets it apart. Enter the Lincoln County Process: a sugar maple charcoal filtration method that imparts a smoother, mellower character and defines Tennessee whiskey's unique identity.

## Is Tennessee Whiskey Just Bourbon by Another Name?

The defining distinction lies in the *Lincoln County Process*, a charcoal filtration method in which the unaged spirit is slowly dripped through sugar maple charcoal before aging. This process, legally required for Tennessee whiskey, imparts a smoother, mellower character that sets it apart from its Kentucky cousin. One exception exists: Benjamin Prichard's, a distillery whose pre–Civil War family recipe earned a legislative exemption in 2013. This historic carveout preserves a distinct lineage within Tennessee whiskey.

Historically, Kentucky came first. By the 1780s and 1790s, settlers in Kentucky were producing corn-based whiskey that evolved into what we now call bourbon. Tennessee's whiskey tradition followed in the early 19th century, culminating in the founding of Jack Daniel's in 1866. While Tennessee has a proud and authentic distilling history, Kentucky's limestone-filtered water, high corn yields, and early innovations in barrel aging gave it a unique edge—establishing it as bourbon's ancestral home.

Still, Tennessee played a formative role in early American distilling. Though Kentucky holds the cultural primacy in bourbon lore, Tennessee whiskey is not an afterthought. It's a regional evolution of a shared American tradition.

This book focuses more heavily on Kentucky not to diminish Tennessee's role, but because Kentucky's unique geological conditions, historical concentration of distilleries, and early innovations gave rise to the spirit that became synonymous with American whiskey: bourbon.

---

*Economic and Cultural Impacts*

As regions developed distinct specialties, markets grew more nuanced and tied to local identities.

By the late 18th century, economic competition had shifted from price to perception. Reputation became the most valuable currency. Consumers began to develop discerning palates, associating specific regions with exceptional quality and distinctive characteristics. This emerging brand loyalty was more than a commercial strategy. It was a form of cultural expression, where the origin of a tobacco leaf or a whiskey batch told a story of local craftsmanship and pride.

The diffusion of tobacco and whiskey culture across the American colonies created a powerful, unifying experience that reached far beyond regional boundaries. Despite distinct local styles, sharing a cigar or whiskey became a unifying social ritual. It was a moment of connection that could bridge differences of class, origin, and background, transforming these products from mere commodities into symbols of shared experience.

This cultural exchange helped forge a shared national identity at a time when the colonies were still discovering their collective voice. Pipe tobacco from Virginia, a whiskey from Pennsylvania: these were not just products but ambassadors of regional character, weaving together the diverse tapestry of emerging American culture. As the 18th century gave way to the 19th, the production of tobacco and whiskey would grow more sophisticated, setting the stage for the rapid expansion ahead.

## V. The Agricultural Revolution in Colonial America

By the mid-18th century, American producers of tobacco and whiskey had moved beyond agricultural experimentation into the realm of refined craft. These products were no longer mere economic lifelines or regional staples. They were being shaped with intentionality, precision, and a growing awareness of brand, flavor, and consumer expectation. This period marked a shift from necessity to connoisseurship, laying the technical and cultural groundwork for national industries that would come to define American identity.

### Tobacco Cultivation in Virginia
Tobacco had long been the backbone of Virginia's economy, but it was during this phase of refinement that cultivation techniques reached new levels of sophistication. Planters invested in highly controlled agricultural methods—from seedbed management to transplanting schedules—to produce uniform and desirable leaves. Curing methods were no longer

improvised; planters became adept at controlling humidity and temperature to maximize aroma, texture, and combustibility.

Colonial authorities established grading systems to standardize quality and reinforce Virginia's reputation in European markets. These systems enabled consumers and brokers to distinguish between regional variants and quality tiers, embedding trust in American-grown tobacco.

Each tobacco leaf became a symbol not only of agricultural success but of precision craftsmanship. As knowledge passed through families and farming communities, tobacco culture evolved into a codified art, rooted in local expertise but shaped by global demand.

While Virginia remained the epicenter of colonial tobacco refinement, other regions began developing their own specialized practices. Notably, in Pennsylvania, Amish and Mennonite communities would later become known for their meticulous cultivation of cigar tobaccos, a parallel tradition rooted in hand labor, soil stewardship, and generational knowledge.

## The Rise and Refinement of Rye Whiskey

In Pennsylvania and Maryland, whiskey production entered a new era of scale and technique. Distillers increasingly prioritized the character of the grain, particularly rye, known for its spiciness and structure. Fermentation and distillation were treated not merely as mechanical steps, but as stages of flavor development. Producers began documenting recipes, refining mash bills, and learning how yeast strains and fermentation time could influence aroma and mouthfeel.

Maryland's distillers added their own twist by crafting smoother, more rounded styles of rye to differentiate from the bolder Pennsylvania expressions. Meanwhile, wood aging transformed from a passive byproduct of storage into a deliberate practice. Barrels—often charred—

were selected and rotated with care to impart depth, vanilla, and smoke.

Larger distilleries emerged by the mid-1700s, connecting local production with expanding markets. These distilleries helped formalize the transition of whiskey from household survival good to regional commercial product. They also played a role in elevating whiskey's cultural role—from farm staple to social centerpiece.

## Bourbon's Emergence in Kentucky

Kentucky's ascension as the heartland of bourbon was the result of both natural bounty and applied knowledge. By the late 18th century, corn had become the grain of choice, not only for its abundance but for the richness it imparted to the final spirit. The state's limestone-filtered water proved ideal for fermentation, while charred oak barrels created the conditions for deep color and layered complexity.

Kentucky's distillers treated whiskey-making as a regional inheritance. Recipes were protected, techniques passed down, and experimentation encouraged. Small-scale producers approached distilling with a reverence for both science and storytelling, crafting spirits that bore the imprint of landscape, lineage, and labor.

By the early 1800s, towns like Bardstown had become centers of both commerce and cultural exchange. Bourbon was more than a drink. It was a product of place, shaped by the distinctive climate, geology, and collective knowledge of Kentucky's early distillers.

---

**The Origins of the Name "Bourbon"**

The name *Bourbon* as applied to whiskey carries both geographical significance and cultural symbolism, rooted in early American gratitude toward France and the regional identity of Kentucky distilling.

*Bourbon County, Kentucky.* Established in 1785 (when Kentucky was still part of Virginia), Bourbon County was named in honor of the French Bourbon dynasty— a tribute to France's critical support during the American Revolutionary War under King Louis XVI. When Kentucky became a state in 1792, Bourbon County remained as one of its original counties. Though not all whiskey came from within its borders, the *Bourbon* name quickly became synonymous with quality Kentucky whiskey, especially from Bardstown and surrounding regions.

*The French Connection.* The House of Bourbon was a major European royal family that ruled France and Spain. Their name entered American geography through places like Bourbon County, KY, and Bourbon Street in New Orleans, both nods to Franco-American alliance. This association gave the term "Bourbon" a sense of prestige and international cultural cachet.

*From County to Cask.* By the early 1800s, Kentucky distillers were shipping corn-based whiskey downriver to New Orleans, where it was marketed as "Old Bourbon." This label referenced both the region of origin and the city's French heritage, making the name commercially and culturally resonant. By the 1820s–1840s, "Bourbon whiskey" was widely recognized as a distinctive style aged in charred oak barrels.

*Why the Name Endured.* "Bourbon" fused geographic identity with historical symbolism. What began as a regional label tied to French-American friendship evolved into the defining name for America's iconic whiskey style, marked by its sweet corn mash, barrel aging, and deep, smooth flavor.

## Toward a National Craft Ethos

What distinguishes this period is not merely volume of production, but the shift toward intentionality. Producers of tobacco and whiskey were no longer just growing crops or distilling grain—they were crafting experiences, identities, and reputations. The rise of grading, branding, and barrel-aging practices signaled a cultural transition in American agriculture: from functional necessity to refined expression.

This craft revolution laid the foundations for the cultural prestige and global demand these products would later command. It also marked the beginning of a distinctly American ethos—one rooted in the transformation of nature through skilled labor, and the elevation of everyday commodities into cultural icons.

## VI. From Home Distillation to a Thriving Industry

By the turn of the 19th century, American whiskey was undergoing a transformation. What began as a frontier craft—rooted in home distillation and necessity—was evolving into a structured, regional industry marked by standardization, specialization, and economic ambition. But this shift also reflected changes in identity. Whiskey was no longer just a practical spirit of survival. It was becoming a commercial product of distinction, regional pride, and national symbolism.

The catalysts for this transition were both material and cultural. As demand increased and transportation networks expanded, distillers moved from informal, small-batch operations to organized commercial enterprises. Quality standards emerged. Techniques were refined. Branding became intentional. And across Kentucky in particular, family-run distilleries laid the foundation for what would soon become the bourbon capital of the world.

### Standardization and Quality Control

As whiskey's role in colonial life expanded, distillers began seeking greater consistency in quality, setting the stage for more formalized production methods.

#### *The Emergence of Quality Standards*

During the late 18th century, American distillers began developing standardized methods to improve consistency and quality:

- **Controlled Fermentation**: Distillers learned to shape fermentation to produce desired flavors. Yeast strains were selected and cultivated with greater precision, enhancing the consistency of batches.
- **Improved Distillation Techniques**: Advances in distillation

technology allowed for more efficient and controlled alcohol production. Artisans perfected methods of heating, cooling, and condensing alcohol vapor to achieve cleaner, more refined spirits.

- **Aging Practices**: Perhaps the most significant innovation was the aging of whiskey in charred oak barrels. This technique, first used as a means of cleaning old barrels, was soon recognized for its ability to enhance flavor and color. By the late 18th century, aging whiskey had become a deliberate and valuable step in the production process.

*Flames kiss the oak, charring barrels to unlock the deep vanilla, spice, and smoke that define bourbon—and echo through the aging of cigars. This fire is not destruction, but transformation.*

*Institutionalization of Whiskey Production*

As the whiskey trade expanded beyond local consumption, distillers began to reimagine their operations with increasing sophistication. Commercial distilleries emerged, signaling a critical shift from household craft to industrial enterprise.

Kentucky rapidly became the epicenter of this whiskey revolution, its unique geographical attributes creating an almost perfect environment for distillation. As previously stated, the state's limestone-filtered water, extraordinarily fertile soil, and abundant corn created a complex ecosystem that would define American whiskey production. This wasn't just an agricultural edge. It was a geological catalyst for a national industry.

Within this expanding landscape, two distinct approaches to whiskey production emerged, each representing a different philosophy of craft. Large-scale commercial distilleries pursued volume and broader market distribution, viewing whiskey as an industrial commodity. Simultaneously, a parallel tradition of small-batch distilleries maintained a more artisanal approach, with craftsmen who viewed whiskey-making as a form of cultural preservation.

These small-batch producers were cultural guardians, emphasizing craftsmanship and quality over mere production efficiency. Each batch embodied inherited craft, building enduring reputations. They maintained traditional techniques even as industrial methods began to dominate, preserving a connection to the earliest days of American distillation.

This growing divide between industrial and craft production widened dramatically in the 1830s with Aeneas Coffey's invention of the continuous still, which fundamentally transformed whiskey production.[2] This innovation made large-scale, consistent production possible, accelerating the divide between industrial and craft approaches. Yet, paradoxically, this very industrialization would later spark a renewed appreciation for small-batch, artisanal methods.

American whiskey evolved amid constant tension: mass production vs. artisanal identity, profit vs. tradition.

---

[2] **Aeneas Coffey (1780–1852)** was an Irish distiller and former excise officer who patented the continuous (or column) still in 1830. His design improved upon earlier models by allowing for continuous distillation and greater efficiency, producing a lighter, more consistent spirit. While initially met with resistance in Ireland and Scotland, the Coffey still was embraced by grain distillers and became foundational to the rise of industrial-scale whiskey production—particularly in America and for blended Scotch.

The commercialization of whiskey production marked a critical transition from informal, local practices to organized industry. As early as the 1790s, distillers began employing consistent branding and marketing strategies to differentiate their whiskey. Labels, trademarks, and advertising were employed to build consumer loyalty and establish market presence.

## Kentucky's Early Bourbon Industry

Kentucky's fertile soil, corn, and limestone water created ideal whiskey conditions. When combined with the emerging practice of aging spirits in charred oak barrels, these elements produced what would become bourbon's distinct American profile.

Family-operated distilleries played a central role in bourbon's early development, passing down recipes and distillation techniques across generations. Bourbon shaped Kentucky's economy and identity, turning towns like Bardstown into cultural hubs.

By the 1840s and 1850s, bourbon had firmly established itself as America's iconic whiskey, symbolizing national craftsmanship and regional pride.

# VII.  Taverns and the Bourbon Economy

As whiskey production expanded throughout the 18th century, the places where it was consumed evolved as well. From the colonial period through the early Republic, taverns served as far more than drinking establishments. They were social institutions where business was conducted, political ideas were debated, and communities formed — and nowhere more so than in Kentucky, where bourbon and tavern culture became deeply intertwined.

### When Was Whiskey First Distilled in Kentucky?

While whiskey was produced in colonial America well before Kentucky's settlement, the Bluegrass State became a distilling powerhouse in the late 18$^{th}$ century. Scots-Irish immigrants brought with them knowledge of distillation and applied it to local corn, giving rise to what would eventually become bourbon.

Though exact dates are debated, whiskey was likely being distilled in Kentucky by the 1780s, with commercial production emerging in the 1790s. One oft-cited figure is Elijah Craig, a Baptist preacher sometimes (mythically) credited with inventing bourbon in 1789 by aging his whiskey in charred oak barrels in what's now Georgetown, KY.

More historically grounded is Jacob Beam, who sold his first barrels of corn whiskey in 1795, founding a lineage that would become Jim Beam. The Corn Patch and Cabin Rights Act of 1776, which offered land incentives for settlers growing corn, helped catalyze this agricultural-to-spirits economy.

By the turn of the 19$^{th}$ century, Kentucky whiskey had begun to distinguish itself—thanks to the region's corn-based mash, limestone-filtered water, and aging practices—marking the beginning of bourbon's formal identity.

## Taverns as Commercial and Political Hubs

Traveling merchants viewed taverns as critical nodes in their economic ecosystems. They were more than rest stops; they were platforms for trade and negotiation. Tavern keepers acted as informal bankers, offering credit, enabling deals, and fostering trust. Their role extended beyond hospitality; they were crucial economic brokers who helped lubricate the wheels of early American trade.

As whiskey's popularity surged during the late 1700s, especially after the Whiskey Rebellion of 1794,[3] taverns became strategic distribution points

---

[3] **The Whiskey Rebellion (1794)** was an armed uprising by frontier distillers in western Pennsylvania protesting a federal excise tax on whiskey imposed in 1791. Many small producers, who relied on whiskey as a form of income and barter, viewed the tax as unjust and discriminatory against rural communities. The rebellion marked one of the first major tests of federal authority under the U.S. Constitution, with President George Washington personally leading militia forces to suppress the revolt—ultimately affirming the power of the federal government to enforce law and taxation.

for regional distilleries. This partnership extended local producers' reach through early supply chains. What began as simple alcohol sales became a complex network of economic exchange, with taverns serving as critical transmission points between producers and consumers.

During periods of economic uncertainty, taverns demonstrated remarkable resilience. They were social anchors where communities could gather, share resources, and collectively strategize in response to external challenges. Before social safety nets, taverns offered mutual aid and problem-solving forums.

The tavern represented a microcosm of early American entrepreneurial spirit: adaptable, multifunctional, and deeply embedded in the social fabric. Each tavern reflected a dynamic, improvised commercial ecosystem.

*Political Forums*

In the realm of politics, taverns in early America were the crucibles of democratic discourse, where the principles of self-governance were forged, debated, and refined. These spaces embodied a radical idea: that political engagement belonged to ordinary citizens, not just elites.

Regular gatherings transformed taverns into informal debating societies. Farmers, merchants, and craftsmen voiced concerns, challenged ideas, and strategized around shared challenges. They were active forums of civic engagement, not passive chats.

Politicians quickly recognized taverns as essential political infrastructure. Campaigns launched over whiskey forged relationships and gauged sentiment. A candidate's credibility was often shaped not by pamphlets but by presence, by how they spoke and listened in these communal spaces.

Tavern networks also served as early information superhighways. News of revolution and elections spread by word of mouth, not print. Travelers and locals alike became messengers, transforming taverns into vibrant nodes of political communication.

More than buildings, these institutions were democratic laboratories. The line between private conversation and public discourse blurred, giving rise to a uniquely American form of civic life: immediate, participatory, and rooted in shared ritual.

## The Old Talbott Tavern – A Case Study

Standing as a living monument to the intricate social and economic web of early American frontier life, the Old Talbott Tavern, established in 1779 in Bardstown[4], embodied the spirit of a nation in formation. More than just a stagecoach stop, it served as a vital nexus of commerce, culture, and community in the Kentucky wilderness, offering travelers, traders, and townsfolk a place where news was exchanged, deals were struck, and the foundations of a regional identity were quietly laid.

**The Old Talbott Tavern in Bardstown, Kentucky** — *Established in 1779, it is considered the oldest western stagecoach stop in America.*

---

[4] **The Old Talbott Tavern**, located in Bardstown, Kentucky, was established in 1779 and is considered the oldest bourbon bar in the United States. It served as a key waypoint for travelers, traders, and political figures—including legends like Daniel Boone and future president Andrew Jackson. Today, it continues to operate as a tavern, inn, and bourbon bar, preserving its legacy as a vital hub of early American social and commercial life.

Strategically positioned along key trade routes, the Old Talbott Tavern quickly became an essential waypoint for a diverse array of travelers. Merchants, politicians, explorers, and adventurers converged within its walls, transforming the tavern from a mere lodging establishment into a dynamic social infrastructure. Its ability to cater to such varied clientele became a testament to the adaptability and entrepreneurial spirit of frontier businesses.

Bourbon production found in the Old Talbott Tavern an unexpected laboratory of innovation. Local distillers used the tavern as an informal testing ground, receiving direct consumer feedback that would help refine recipes and improve quality. Visitors would purchase bourbon to carry on their travels, inadvertently creating an early form of marketing that spread the reputation of Kentucky whiskey far beyond its geographic origins.

The tavern's walls bore witness to significant moments of political and cultural discourse. Legendary figures like Daniel Boone walked its floors, and future presidents engaged in conversations that would shape the emerging identity of Kentucky and the broader American frontier. These exchanges actively shaped regional and national identity.

As a cultural institution, the Old Talbott Tavern transcended its immediate commercial function. It became a repository of collective memory, a space where individual stories intersected with broader historical narratives. Its endurance—remaining one of the oldest operating taverns in America—is a powerful testament to the deep, intricate connections between bourbon culture, social history, and the persistent spirit of American entrepreneurship.

The tavern's legacy is not simply about preservation, but about continuous transformation. Each generation added to its story, making the Old Talbott Tavern a living chronicle of Kentucky's bourbon culture. In a broader sense, taverns across the state functioned as crucibles of experimentation, reputation, and identity. Word-of-mouth replaced marketing. Bourbon wasn't just poured. It was tested, judged, and embedded into community memory. In these spaces, Kentucky whiskey became more than a product. It became culture.

## VIII. The Science of Kentucky's Limestone Water

Among the many factors contributing to bourbon's unique character, one of the most important is the region's limestone-filtered water. This natural resource provides ideal conditions for bourbon production, enhancing everything from fermentation to flavor profile. Understanding the science behind Kentucky's limestone water is essential for appreciating why the state remains synonymous with bourbon.

### Mineral Filtration

The limestone aquifer system naturally filters Kentucky's water, significantly enhancing bourbon's flavor. Limestone blocks iron, bourbon's worst contaminant. Iron taints flavor, disrupts aging, and discolors the final product.

The purity provided by this natural filtration process is one of the primary reasons bourbon distillers have historically clustered in Kentucky. The filtered water ensures that the foundational ingredient in bourbon-making—water itself—contributes positively to the final product's taste, consistency, and clarity. Without this natural edge, early Kentucky bourbon wouldn't have reached such quality or acclaim.

### *Mineral Enhancement*

Filtration matters, but limestone also enriches the water. The limestone aquifer, in fact, enriches the water with beneficial minerals, particularly calcium and magnesium, which are crucial to bourbon production. Water passing through limestone absorbs minerals that enhance fermentation.

Calcium supports yeast health, boosting fermentation. The presence of calcium helps maintain robust yeast populations, ensuring efficient conversion of sugars to alcohol. Improved fermentation lets bourbon express its full sweetness and complexity.

Magnesium nourishes yeast, aiding fermentation. Its presence promotes consistent alcohol production, enhancing both the quality and the efficiency of the distillation process. Together, these minerals create ideal yeast conditions for consistent flavor.

These minerals shape bourbon chemistry beyond fermentation. During distillation, minerals help separate compounds, deepening character and shaping bourbon.

## pH Balance and Its Effects

Another critical factor contributing to bourbon's unique character is the naturally balanced pH of Kentucky's limestone-filtered water. Water drawn from these limestone aquifers generally maintains a pH level between 6.5 and 8.5. This slightly alkaline nature provides several advantages throughout the bourbon-making process.

pH balance first impacts the mashing stage. During this process, grains are cooked and combined with water to convert starches into fermentable sugars. Optimal pH improves starch breakdown and boosts alcohol yield.

The influence of pH balance continues during fermentation, where yeast activity thrives in slightly alkaline conditions. Kentucky's natural pH supports yeast and ensures flavor consistency.

The impact of pH levels also extends to the aging process. During barrel aging, the interaction between alcohol and charred oak is influenced by the acidity or alkalinity of the spirit. A well-balanced pH enhances the extraction of desirable flavor compounds from the wood, contributing to bourbon's complexity and smoothness. Bourbon's mellow depth owes much to Kentucky's natural pH.

## Modern Analysis and Relevance to Bourbon Production

Modern testing has validated the distillers' early observations about limestone-filtered water. Recent studies have demonstrated that the limestone-filtered water of Kentucky consistently exhibits optimal characteristics for bourbon production.

Analysis of the water's mineral content shows that it contains significant levels of calcium and magnesium while maintaining minimal iron content, typically measured at less than 0.1 parts per million. Minimal iron prevents unwanted reactions during fermentation and aging. The water's consistent mineral content ensures reliable, uniform flavor.

Controlled experiments have been conducted to compare various water sources for bourbon production, and Kentucky's natural limestone-filtered water consistently emerges as superior. Modern systems mimic Kentucky's water but can't replicate its exact mineral profile. The unique combination of purity, mineral content, and pH balance remains a defining element of traditional bourbon production.

The significance of this natural resource has not been lost on bourbon producers. Many distilleries continue to emphasize their access to Kentucky's limestone-filtered water as a critical aspect of their branding, appealing to both tradition and scientific validation. For consumers, Kentucky's water enhances bourbon's romance and sense of place.

As bourbon production grew, this natural advantage became crucial. Yet, the influence of bourbon and cigars on American culture was not limited to their production alone. These industries soon reshaped American society, transforming colonial goods into cultural symbols.

## Conclusion: From Colonial Roots to Cultural Symbols

The intertwined rise of tobacco and whiskey in early America laid the foundation for two of the nation's most enduring cultural icons. From John Rolfe's pioneering tobacco cultivation to the distillation expertise of Scottish and Irish immigrants, this first luxury pairing emerged through a blend of innovation, adaptation, and cross-cultural exchange. What began as economic necessity soon evolved into expressions of identity, ritual, and status.

Their influence extended beyond the marketplace. In taverns and salons, on plantations and political stages, bourbon and cigars shaped rituals of belonging, reinforced social hierarchies, and served as instruments of persuasion and power. They weren't just products. They were performances of American life.

This transformation would only deepen in the 19th century, when bourbon and cigars became hallmarks of prestige, connoisseurship, and national identity. The next chapter explores this Golden Age, when these artisanal goods ascended from regional traditions to icons of American refinement and aspiration.

CHAPTER 2

# The Golden Age

*Bourbon, Cigars & the 19th-Century Boom*

T he 19th century marked a Golden Age for both bourbon and cigars. Industrial innovation, expanding trade networks, and a growing national appetite for luxury goods transformed each from a regional commodity into a parallel narrative of sophistication, craftsmanship, and American identity.

## IV.   Bourbon: America's Frontier Spirit

During the early 1800s, particularly following the Louisiana Purchase,[5] bourbon evolved from a frontier curiosity into America's quintessential spirit. The Mississippi River, initially navigated by flatboats and notably enhanced by the advent of steamboat travel in the early 1800s, became vital for transporting bourbon barrels from Kentucky's heartland to distant markets, especially New Orleans.

---

[5] **The Louisiana Purchase of 1803** was a land deal between the United States and France, in which the U.S. acquired approximately 828,000 square miles of territory west of the Mississippi River—doubling the nation's size and opening vast new frontiers for settlement, agriculture, and commerce.

*The Mississippi River Trade Network*

Bourbon shipments initially relied on flatboats—simple, disposable vessels floated downriver and dismantled upon arrival, which were inexpensive but limited in capacity. The introduction of steamboat travel, marked by the 1811 maiden voyage of the *New Orleans*, revolutionized river commerce. By the 1820s, steamboats allowed for larger, more efficient shipments of bourbon barrels, which were now stacked high and transported swiftly down the Mississippi to meet the growing demand. Once docked in cities like New Orleans, the barrels were sold to merchants, taverns, and distributors eager to satisfy the public's appetite for this distinctively American spirit.

New Orleans quickly became a central hub for bourbon distribution. Its status as a commercial and cultural crossroads lent credibility and prestige to bourbon, transforming it from a regional product into a cultural symbol. The city's diverse population—comprising French, Spanish, Creole, and American influences—enthusiastically embraced bourbon as part of its vibrant social scene. From exclusive private clubs to bustling public taverns, bourbon became a staple of both celebration and daily life.

The Mississippi River trade network established bourbon's reputation as America's frontier spirit. Its association with New Orleans, coupled with its rugged, bold character, appealed to those who saw bourbon as a symbol of resilience and authenticity.

*Industrialization and Distillation Innovations*

The 19th century marked a period of significant technological innovation in bourbon production. As distillation techniques improved and industrialization took hold, bourbon evolved from a local specialty to a commercial commodity with a national and international reputation.

Central to this transformation was the standardization of bourbon production, which involved refining distillation methods, enhancing aging techniques, and ensuring product consistency. Improved copper stills allowed for greater control over the distillation process, resulting in a cleaner and higher-quality product. Additionally, the importance of aging bourbon in charred oak barrels—widely adopted by distillers by the 1820s—dramatically enhanced its flavor profile and aesthetic qualities.

This practice of intentionally aging bourbon in charred oak barrels was discovered to mellow and enhance the whiskey's flavor, imparting notes of vanilla, caramel, and spice. Over time, this maturation process became a hallmark of bourbon production, distinguishing it from other spirits and contributing to its emerging reputation for quality and depth.

As bourbon's craftsmanship evolved, so too did the need for protecting and standardizing its presentation. In 1870, Old Forester revolutionized the industry by becoming the first bourbon brand sold exclusively in sealed glass bottles, a move that ensured consistency and authenticity while signaling a new era of consumer trust. By coupling aged flavor with reliable packaging, bourbon was repositioned as a refined, premium product worthy of national distinction.[6]

This evolution laid the groundwork for the rise of iconic distilleries such as Old Forester, Old Crow, and Old Taylor — names that would come to define the American whiskey landscape. But the 19th century also gave rise to many other producers—some still thriving, others long vanished—that helped forge bourbon's legacy. The following snapshot highlights both the enduring institutions and the forgotten pioneers that shaped the Golden Age of American whiskey.

## Legacy Distilleries — Icons That Endured and Legends That Faded

The 19th century saw the emergence of bourbon producers that would shape American whiskey for generations. Some have become enduring institutions. Others—despite their prominence—faded into obscurity. Together, they forged the Golden Age of bourbon.

---

[6] **Old Forester's** bottled bourbon, introduced by George Garvin Brown in 1870, was a milestone in bourbon history, marking the industry's transition toward modern branding and distribution standards.

**Foundational Distilleries Still Operating Today**

- Buffalo Trace (site dating to 1775): Distilling on the site dates to 1775, with the modern Buffalo Trace Distillery name adopted in 1999 after major restoration. A pioneer in both heritage and experimentation.
- Old Forester (est. 1870): First bourbon sold exclusively in sealed glass bottles, setting a new standard of quality and consistency.
- Maker's Mark (est. 1953): Introduced in 1953, revived the historic Burks' Distillery with a smooth wheated bourbon and its iconic red wax seal.
- Jim Beam (est. 1795): A global household name, known for its resilience through war, Prohibition, and changing consumer tastes.
- Wild Turkey (est. 1940): Famous for high-proof, full-bodied expressions and its cult following among bourbon purists. The Wild Turkey brand was introduced in 1940, building on distilling traditions dating back to the late 19th century.
- Heaven Hill (est. 1935): Still family-owned and home to brands like Elijah Craig and Evan Williams.

**Distilleries That Disappeared — But Helped Build the Legacy**

- Old Crow Distillery (Frankfort, KY): Once among the most respected producers; fell into decline and ceased operations in the 1980s.
- Old Taylor Distillery (Frankfort, KY): Founded by bourbon pioneer E.H. Taylor; shuttered for decades before being reborn as Castle & Key.
- Atherton Distillery (Athertonville, KY): A dominant force in LaRue County's economy until a 1972 fire and market shifts ended its run.
- James M. Stone Distillery (Scott County, KY): While not widely remembered today, the James M. Stone Distillery was listed among the largest whiskey producers in Scott County in 19th-century tax records and regional economic surveys.
- C.L. Applegate & Co. (Yelvington, KY): A 19th-century distillery that declined amid consolidation pressures and resource constraints.

These names—whether still thriving or long forgotten—represent the roots of America's bourbon story. Some became pillars of modern whiskey culture; others are etched only in labels, ruins, or lore. But all of them shaped the character, flavor, and mythos of the spirit we know today.

---

By the end of the 19th century, bourbon had transcended its regional roots to become a symbol of American ingenuity and tradition. It was no longer a local commodity. It was a cultural artifact representing the frontier spirit of the nation itself.

As bourbon's status grew, so too did the market for premium cigars. The next section will explore how the cigar industry experienced its own Golden Age during this period and how bourbon and cigars became intertwined symbols of leisure, sophistication, and cultural identity.

# II. The Growth of American Cigar Tobacco

As bourbon was elevated from barrel to bottle, cigars were likewise undergoing their own transformation—from farm to factory, leaf to luxury.

### The Connecticut River Valley: America's Cigar Tobacco Heartland

The Connecticut River Valley became the epicenter of American cigar tobacco cultivation during the 19th century. The region's fertile soil, humid climate, and long growing season made it ideal for producing high-quality tobacco leaves, most notably Connecticut Shade and Broadleaf tobacco.

*Connecticut Shade*

The innovation of growing Connecticut Shade tobacco began in the late 1800s when farmers started using cheesecloth tents to shield crops from direct sunlight. This method produced leaves that were thinner, lighter in color, and more elastic, qualities that made them ideal for use as high-quality cigar wrappers. The delicate flavor profile of Connecticut Shade tobacco became synonymous with luxury cigars, both domestically and internationally.

*Broadleaf Tobacco*

By contrast, Broadleaf tobacco was grown without shade tents, resulting in leaves that were thicker, darker, and stronger in flavor. Its robust character made it a popular choice for binder and filler tobacco, as well as for cigars emphasizing bold, earthy flavors.

Both varieties flourished throughout the 19th century, with Connecticut farmers continuously refining their curing and fermentation processes to enhance flavor and durability. By the late 1800s, Connecticut Shade and Broadleaf tobaccos were widely regarded as among the finest in the world, contributing significantly to the cultural perception of cigars as markers of success.

## Other Regional Tobacco Traditions: Pennsylvania and Beyond

While the Connecticut River Valley dominated the premium wrapper market, other American regions also contributed significantly to the cigar tobacco economy during the 19th century. Chief among them was Pennsylvania, where Lancaster County emerged as a central hub for the cultivation of cigar filler and binder leaves. Pennsylvania Broadleaf, known for its dark, rich flavor and excellent burning qualities, became a popular choice for cigars aimed at both domestic and export markets.

This region's success owed much to the deep agricultural knowledge of its communities—including the Amish, whose disciplined, sustainable farming practices helped elevate tobacco into one of the county's most profitable and stable crops. Their careful crop rotation, organic fertilization, and hands-on approach to curing and sorting lent a distinctive quality to Lancaster-grown tobacco, reinforcing its status within the American cigar tradition.

Other regions, such as southern Maryland and parts of Ohio's Miami Valley, also contributed to the national supply chain, though often at smaller scales. Each brought its own soil composition, climatic influence, and farming tradition, expanding the geographic diversity of American cigar tobacco.

**Plain People, Fine Tobacco — The Amish and the Lancaster Tobacco Legacy**

While cigar factories in cities like Tampa and New York drove industrial-scale production in the late 19th century, Lancaster County, Pennsylvania, became a quieter hub of tobacco cultivation, thanks in large part to its Amish and Mennonite farming communities.

By the mid-1800s, these groups were growing and curing Pennsylvania Broadleaf tobacco, a thick, hearty variety prized for its use in cigar wrappers and filler. Though the Amish do not smoke or use tobacco themselves—due to religious prohibitions—they played a crucial role in its cultivation. Tobacco farming became a mainstay of Lancaster agriculture, with families carefully managing seedbeds, hand-harvesting leaves, and hanging them in distinctive wooden barns for curing.

While the Amish did not typically manufacture cigars themselves, the tobacco they produced supplied nearby towns and regional factories where hand-rolled cigars were made. Their emphasis on precision, discipline, and non-mechanized labor contributed to Lancaster County's reputation for producing some of the finest domestic cigar tobacco in the country.

Today, Lancaster's cigar tobacco legacy endures, with Amish farms continuing to grow premium leaf for niche markets. This unique collaboration between religious tradition and commercial agriculture remains a powerful example of how even communities that abstain from tobacco use have shaped America's cigar story.

# Industrialization of Cigar Production

By the 1880s, mechanization transformed cigar manufacturing, allowing companies to produce cigars faster and more cheaply than ever before. This mass production expanded market access, driving down prices and bringing cigars into the hands of a growing middle class. To preserve a sense of exclusivity amid this scale, manufacturers emphasized quality control, consistent branding, and ornate packaging, elevating cigar boxes and bands into symbols of refinement and identity. As the industry evolved, a handful of influential brands—both domestic pioneers and prestigious imports—came to define the era's new cigar economy.

The rise of these brands was not just a story of marketing and luxury. It reshaped local economies. Cities like New York, Tampa, and Key West became thriving cigar production centers, attracting thousands of skilled rollers, many of them immigrants from Cuba, Spain, and Eastern Europe. Entire neighborhoods were shaped by the rhythms of cigar work, from leaf sorting to hand-rolling to box pressing.

## Icons of the 19th-Century Cigar Boom

As cigar manufacturing industrialized in the United States, a new class of influential brands emerged—especially in cities like Key West, Tampa, and New York—bringing scale, style, and sophistication to the evolving industry. These American producers helped establish cigars as both accessible luxuries and cultural symbols, even as select Cuban imports maintained their global prestige.

### Pioneering American Manufacturers

- **E. H. Gato (est. 1874, Florida)**: A Cuban immigrant and trailblazer in Southern cigar production, Gato brought large-scale manufacturing to Key West, helping define Florida's role in the national cigar economy.
- **Bock & Co. (est. 1860s, New York)**: Among the first to use ornate cigar bands, Bock elevated packaging into an art form and set trends that competitors followed nationwide.
- **Garcia y Vega (est. 1882)**: Known for quality and later for innovation in machine-rolled cigars, Garcia y Vega bridged the gap between artisanal tradition and industrial efficiency.
- **La Flor de Cuba (est. 1876)**: Though associated with Cuban tobacco, this brand became one of the earliest to explicitly align itself with American notions of luxury through bold branding and romanticized imagery.

### Imports That Shaped Prestige

- **H. Upmann (est. 1844, Havana)**: One of the first Cuban brands to associate cigars with financial and social status, becoming a benchmark for premium perception.
- **El Rey del Mundo (est. 1848, Havana)**: A globally recognized Cuban label, famed for its craftsmanship and appeal to elite international consumers.
- **Hoyo de Monterrey (est. 1865, Havana)**: Revered for its balanced flavor and refined presentation, Hoyo reinforced the mystique of Cuban cigars in elite American markets.

Together, these producers—both domestic innovators and influential imports—shaped a new kind of cigar economy in 19th-century America, where branding, symbolism, and scalable production merged to redefine the meaning of luxury.

---

Yet, mechanization did not spell the end for hand-rolled cigars. Instead, it led to a bifurcated industry where machine-made cigars catered to mass-market consumption, while premium, hand-rolled cigars continued to represent luxury and craftsmanship. This dynamic allowed the cigar industry to appeal to a broad spectrum of consumers, from working-class laborers to high-society elites.

> For a comprehensive and detailed examination of the growth of the American cigar industry during this period, see *America's Cigar Story: The History, Politics, and Legacy of Cigars from 1762 to the Modern Era* (Saviano, 2025).

**The Sanchez & Haya Cigar Factory, Ybor City, Tampa** – *A cornerstone of America's cigar heritage, where immigrant craftsmanship and industrial ambition rolled side by side to shape the "Cigar Capital of the World."*

As industrialization reshaped cigar production and distribution, bourbon continued its parallel rise, with the two industries increasingly intertwined as symbols of leisure, luxury, and American identity during the 19th-century boom.

## III. Bourbon and Cigars as Symbols of Prestige and Leisure

As bourbon and cigars each solidified their reputations as luxury commodities throughout the 19th century, they became intertwined as complementary symbols of sophistication, leisure, and power. This cultural convergence was not accidental but rather the result of deliberate branding, social practices, and the influence of popular culture. From exclusive private clubs to mainstream media, the pairing of bourbon and cigars became a cultural statement that endured well into the 20th century.

### Private Clubs and Gentlemen's Lounges

The association of bourbon and cigars with prestige and leisure was perhaps most visible in the exclusive private clubs and gentlemen's lounges that proliferated during the 19th century. These establishments were not simply social venues; they were bastions of elite culture where business negotiations, political discussions, and social rituals were conducted over glasses of fine bourbon and premium cigars.

The appeal of bourbon and cigars in these settings was twofold: they were both status symbols and social lubricants. Historical accounts from the period indicate that the enjoyment of these luxuries was ritualized, involving particular methods of preparation, consumption, and appreciation. Whether it was the deliberate process of lighting and drawing on a hand-rolled cigar or the meticulous pouring of aged bourbon into crystal glassware, the experience was meant to be savored and displayed.

Private clubs such as New York City's Union Club (established in 1836) and the Metropolitan Club (founded in 1891 by J.P. Morgan and other powerful industrialists) became renowned for their cigar lounges and whiskey selections. These clubs were symbols of exclusivity and sophistication, where powerful businessmen, politicians, and cultural elites forged connections over bourbon and cigars.

By the 1880s, cigar manufacturers such as A. T. Beck & Co. in New York—mirroring the practices of elite European firms like J. Frankau & Co.[7]—were producing custom blends for private clubs and exclusive clientele. Bourbon, already esteemed for its aging process and bold flavor profile, had by then secured its place alongside cigars as a premium indulgence of the American elite.

The very act of sharing a cigar or bourbon drink with colleagues or clients communicated social status and cultural knowledge. Moreover, the rituals surrounding their consumption reinforced a sense of exclusivity and tradition, qualities that were increasingly commodified by manufacturers keen to promote their products as essential elements of an elite lifestyle.

While private clubs provided controlled environments for the appreciation of bourbon and cigars, popular culture would soon take this pairing beyond the confines of exclusivity, embedding it more broadly within American leisure culture.

## Cultural Convergence and Branding

The intertwined appeal of bourbon and cigars did not remain confined to the social elite. By the late 19th century, particularly during the Gilded Age, the cultural prestige associated with these products began to spread, in part due to the efforts of advertisers, brand strategists, and media

---

[7] **A. T. Beck & Co.**, a New York-based cigar house active in the late 19th century, was known for its bespoke blends crafted for high-end clientele, particularly in social clubs and elite circles. Its approach mirrored that of J. Frankau & Co., a distinguished London firm founded in the early 1800s, which served as the exclusive importer of Havana cigars to Britain and specialized in supplying custom-labeled cigars to aristocratic and private club markets. Together, these firms exemplify the convergence of craftsmanship and social exclusivity in the emerging luxury cigar economy.

representations that sought to align bourbon and cigars with broader concepts of leisure, masculinity, and success.

Advertising campaigns often framed bourbon and cigars as markers of accomplishment, meant to be enjoyed by those who had achieved a certain level of success. Print advertisements, especially those appearing in publications such as *Harper's Weekly* and *The Saturday Evening Post*, depicted sophisticated gentlemen enjoying cigars and bourbon in refined settings. The image of the self-made man relishing a cigar and bourbon in his study became a powerful cultural motif, symbolizing both personal achievement and refined taste.

Manufacturers themselves began to actively promote the compatibility of their products. Bourbon producers increasingly suggested that their spirits were best enjoyed with a fine cigar, while cigar manufacturers reciprocated by recommending bourbon as the ideal complement to their offerings. This strategic branding forged a powerful association that persists to this day.

Public figures such as Mark Twain and Ulysses S. Grant—both known for their fondness for cigars and whiskey—contributed to the cultural mythos of these goods as emblems of power and refinement. Grant's legendary cigar consumption during the Civil War helped solidify the cigar as a symbol of authority and masculine endurance.

**Women & the Gilded Age: Quiet Participants in a Masculine Ritual**

While bourbon and cigars were largely marketed as emblems of masculinity during the 19th century, women were not wholly absent from this culture. In elite circles and bohemian salons, women occasionally participated in cigar smoking and whiskey tasting, often as acts of transgression or symbols of sophistication.

Illustrated in period literature, advertisements, and social commentary, such moments signaled shifting gender norms beneath the surface of a male-dominated leisure culture. Female cigar smokers appeared in satirical illustrations and, increasingly, as symbolic figures in cigar advertisements—part muse, part marketing device.

Though rare, these instances prefigured the more visible role women would play in both industries in the 20th century, as consumers, tastemakers, and cultural icons. The imagery of the era reflected this complexity. Advertisements became not just promotional tools but cultural mirrors, capturing the aspirational codes, gendered aesthetics, and symbolic weight cigars carried in the American imagination.

---

### VISUAL ARCHIVE: Gilded Age Cigar Culture in Print

These images offer a window into how cigars were marketed not only as products, but as cultural statements, infused with gender roles, patriotic motifs, and aspirational luxury.

**"Take It Easy – S.A.": Leisure and Masculinity in Early Tobacco Advertising (c. 1863)**
*This Civil War–era tobacco label depicts a relaxed, well-dressed man smoking a cigar, presenting tobacco use as a marker of leisure, composure, and masculine self-possession.*

**"Two Friends" Cigar Label, circa 1890**

*This original chromolithographic cigar label, titled "Two Friends," was produced around 1890 and exemplifies the intricate and artistic designs used in cigar marketing during the late 19th century. The label features a Victorian-era woman shaking hands with a Saint Bernard dog, symbolizing companionship and trust. Such imagery was common in cigar advertising, aiming to associate the product with positive emotions and refined aesthetics. The use of embossing and vibrant colors reflects the high production values and competitive nature of cigar branding at the time.*

**"Yankee Girl" Cigar Advertisement, circa 1890s**

*This vibrant lithographic sign features a young woman dressed in patriotic attire, promoting the "Yankee Girl" cigar brand. Such imagery reflects the era's marketing strategies that intertwined national pride with feminine allure, aiming to broaden the appeal of cigars beyond traditional male consumers. The use of a female figure in cigar advertising during this period signifies the subtle shifts in societal norms and the* emerging visibility of women in public and commercial spheres.

# Perfection of Whiskey.

ABSOLUTELY PURE.

ABSOLUTELY PURE.

TRADE

BELLE OF NELSON OLD FASHIONED HAND MADE SOUR MASH WHISKEY

MARK

A Pure and Fine Kentucky Whiskey, **distilled in the hills of Nelson County** from the finest of Golden Rye-malt and Maize and Mountain Spring Water. Our oldest stock, distilled in 1875, is cased. Each case containing two gallons, at **$15.00** per case. Established 1845. Refer to all Louisville Banking Institutions. Orders filled from New York, Boston, Philadelphia, San Francisco, New Orleans, Birmingham, Atlanta, Ft. Worth, Ocala, Fla., or Denver Depots. If this is not satisfactory, address Belle of Nelson Dist. Co., Louisville, Ky., and your orders will have prompt attention. Cases sent on trial, and can be returned at our expense if not as represented.

This Whiskey is cased especially for those who need Whiskey AS A MEDICINE OR BEVERAGE, and all such can get it at FIRST HANDS STRICTLY PURE.

### BARTLEY, JOHNSON & CO., Louisville, Ky.

Yes, every man has his price, but he can't make his grocer agree with him.—*Columbus Post.*

**"Perfection of Whiskey" Advertisement, Bartley, Johnson & Co., Louisville, KY, 1875**

*This advertisement exemplifies the burgeoning branding strategies of the late 19th century, positioning Kentucky bourbon as a symbol of purity and tradition. The imagery and language used reflect the era's emphasis on quality and authenticity in spirits marketing.*

Advertisements from the mid- to late 19th century, as seen in the Visual Archive above, reflect the evolving cultural narrative surrounding cigars in American life—where leisure, craftsmanship, status, and symbolism intersected in increasingly sophisticated visual forms.

## IV. New Orleans as a Cultural Confluence

New Orleans was where bourbon's frontier journey ended and its cosmopolitan rise began. The city's geographic position, layered cultural identity, and economic importance made it a natural meeting ground for the bourbon trade and the cigar economy, turning consumption into ritual and commerce into spectacle.

### Trade, Culture, and Social Life

Already established as a bourbon gateway by mid-century, New Orleans became the ritual and symbolic stage for its elevation into high society.

The Mississippi River was a cultural artery, linking frontier production with cosmopolitan demand. By the mid-1800s, New Orleans ranked among the busiest ports in the world, attracting merchants, planters, sailors, and socialites. For distillers, the city offered not only access to international markets but also a stage upon which bourbon could ascend from backcountry staple to symbol of elevated taste.

The rise of dedicated cigar lounges and bourbon bars in the late 19th century further contributed to the pairing's cultural visibility. By the 1880s, even established venues like the St. Charles Hotel—which had long been a symbol of refined Southern hospitality—began creating specialized spaces, such as its Cigar and Bourbon Room (opened 1882), to showcase these luxuries in a more curated, public-facing manner. Unlike the tightly restricted gentlemen's clubs of New York, these settings invited a broader clientele while still maintaining the aesthetic of sophistication. They helped normalize the ritual of pairing bourbon and cigars outside elite circles, transforming it into a wider cultural practice.

MEN'S CAFE                                    BILLIARD ROOM

**Interior of the Men's Café and Billiard Room, St. Charles Hotel, circa 1917**
*This lavish social space exemplified the elegance of New Orleans' elite hospitality culture, where bourbon and cigars were not only consumed but ritualized. Settings like this helped cement the pairing as a symbol of refinement, masculinity, and leisure in the late 19th and early 20th centuries.*

This culture of enjoyment—expressed through Mardi Gras festivities, political salons, and high-society soirées—centered on visible, performative consumption. The selection, presentation, and pairing of bourbon and cigars became signifiers of class and taste. And practically, bourbon's resilience in transport and bold barrel-aged profile made it especially well-suited to the demands and palate of the city's diverse population.

Yet it was not only bourbon's arrival that marked New Orleans' importance—it was also the city's function as a Caribbean gateway that gave rise to a singular fusion of American and Cuban luxury traditions.

## Integration of Cuban Cigars

Through its seaport connections to Havana and the broader Caribbean, New Orleans became a key conduit for Cuban cigars—widely regarded by the mid-19<sup>th</sup> century as the finest in the world. These cigars arrived not just as goods, but as symbols of worldliness, political intrigue, and artisanal prestige.

Among the city's mercantile elite, smoking a Cuban cigar alongside a well-aged bourbon became a social ritual, an act that conferred both status and cultural literacy. Cuban cigars gained such popularity in New Orleans that the city was often referred to as the cigar capital of the American South.

Cigar shops, smoking lounges, and tobacco emporiums spread across the French Quarter and into the burgeoning commercial districts of New Orleans, including what would later be known as the Central Business District. These venues were more than retail outlets. They served as dynamic gathering spaces for professionals, politicians, and artists, where news was exchanged, reputations forged, and deals sealed over shared cigars.

The influx of Cuban expatriates—some fleeing political unrest, others seeking economic opportunity—added further depth to the city's cigar culture. They brought expertise in rolling, fermenting, and blending, but also their own stories, music, and culinary traditions, further enriching the city's hybrid identity.

This convergence of Caribbean cigar craftsmanship and American whiskey production was more than a commercial pairing; it was a cultural alliance. Distillers began promoting cigars as natural companions to their bourbon, creating a sensory experience that appealed to a growing class of American connoisseurs.

Meanwhile, American-grown tobacco—especially from the Connecticut River Valley and Pennsylvania's Lancaster County—began carving out a place in the luxury market. While Cuban cigars still reigned supreme, these domestic varieties increasingly found their way into premium blends sold in New Orleans' most prestigious cigar shops.

In this way, New Orleans became not only a center of distribution, but a crucible of innovation and prestige. The city's cigar and bourbon rituals helped codify a new language of leisure, one that would ripple outward into the American imagination.

As the 19th century gave way to the 20th, this cultural synergy would evolve further, facing both opportunity and disruption. Yet the blueprint for pairing American bourbon with world-class cigars—rooted in the streets, salons, and smoky parlors of New Orleans and beyond—would remain a lasting legacy of the Golden Age.

# V. Economic and Social Impact of the Golden Age

The Golden Age of bourbon and cigars coincided with a revolution in American transportation. The rise of railroads and steamboats dramatically expanded distribution, allowing regional goods to reach urban centers and national markets for the first time.

Bourbon's early expansion relied heavily on the Mississippi River, which connected Kentucky distillers to major southern ports like New Orleans. From there, barrels were redistributed along inland and coastal trade routes to reach eastern cities. This network helped bourbon evolve from a local staple into a national symbol of craftsmanship and character.

Cigars followed a parallel trajectory. By the 1850s and 1860s, railroads carried tobacco from Connecticut and Pennsylvania to factories in New York, Key West, and Tampa, supporting mass production and widening distribution.

As noted earlier, Cuban imports—especially brands like H. Upmann and El Rey del Mundo—continued to define international luxury, but American producers increasingly shaped the domestic market, blending accessibility with sophistication.

*Regional Markets and Expanding Commerce*

As demand grew, new infrastructure emerged. Louisville, Chicago, and Cincinnati joined New Orleans as major bourbon hubs. Meanwhile, New York, Tampa, and Key West developed as cigar production centers, each with its own manufacturing style and cultural flavor.

This regional diversification helped bourbon and cigars transcend elite consumption. As the American middle class expanded, these goods became attainable symbols of taste and upward mobility. Whether poured in a private club or smoked on a workingman's porch, bourbon and cigars blurred the lines between luxury and accessibility.

*Economic Implications of Expanding Markets*

Meeting this demand required scaling. As shown earlier in this chapter, bourbon producers refined aging and bottling, while cigar manufacturers adopted mechanization in the 1880s. Both industries balanced industrial scale with artisanal identity, preserving the prestige of premium hand-rolled cigars and barrel-aged bourbons even as production expanded.

> For a detailed account of these developments, see *America's Cigar Story: The History, Politics, and Legacy of Cigars from 1762 to the Modern Era* (Saviano, 2025).

## Cultural Identity and National Pride

The ascent of bourbon and cigars was more than economic. It was symbolic. Unlike imported luxuries, these products reflected American ingenuity, place-based pride, and cultural narrative.

Bourbon embodied frontier independence and self-reliance. Its bold profile and rustic origins resonated with a nation forging its own identity. Cigars, once elite indulgences, became tools of personal branding that signaled taste, accomplishment, and social ascent. Connecticut and

Pennsylvania tobaccos began to rival imports, helping domestic products anchor American definitions of luxury.

By the late 19th century, several American whiskey and bourbon distilleries actively embraced cigars in their marketing and brand environments. *Old Crow* and *Old Forester*, for example, were among the spirits often advertised alongside cigars in gentlemen's clubs and hotel lounges. These establishments—common in cities like Louisville, Cincinnati, and New Orleans—routinely offered cigars with featured house bourbons as part of an all-American experience. In some cases, saloons and rail lines even created proprietary cigar labels tied to regional bourbon brands. The *Stitzel Brothers*, precursors to *Stitzel-Weller*, promoted their whiskey in retail spaces that also sold imported and domestic cigars, positioning both as hallmarks of refined masculine leisure.

*Rituals, Hospitality, and Belonging*

By the late 19th century, offering a guest a glass of bourbon or a fine cigar had become an act of cultural literacy. These goods shaped the rituals of American hospitality at once refined and relational, woven into the choreography of saloons, drawing rooms, and hotel lounges. Their significance lay not only in taste but in symbolism: success, trust, and distinction. Early distilleries often hosted tastings or operated barrooms where cigars were available for purchase or complimentary enjoyment. Brands like *Cascade Whiskey* (which would later evolve into George Dickel) were regularly advertised in tandem with cigars in late 19th-century newspapers. Together, bourbon and cigars helped define an American code of welcome, evoking both democratic access and aspirational refinement.

## Tennessee Whiskey: Bourbon Before the Split

For much of the 19th century, what we now call Tennessee whiskey was often marketed—and perceived—as a regional variety of bourbon. Tennessee distillers used similar mash bills, charred oak aging, and grain sourcing as their Kentucky counterparts. The federal government had yet to define bourbon formally, so the distinction between Kentucky and Tennessee whiskey remained blurry.

Newspapers and trade advertisements from cities like St. Louis, Nashville, and Memphis frequently grouped Tennessee whiskey under the general category of "fine bourbons." This practice was especially common in shipping hubs and along trade routes, where Kentucky and Tennessee products were often sold side by side. In effect, "bourbon" functioned as both a stylistic description and a marketing shorthand, rather than a strict geographical designation.

This branding ambiguity persisted well into the late 19th century. It wasn't until the rise of Jack Daniel's in the early 20th century—and the formalization of the Lincoln County Process as a defining feature of Tennessee whiskey—that a clear commercial and legal split began to emerge. Federal legislation such as the Bottled-in-Bond Act (1897) and the Pure Food and Drug Act (1906) further codified production standards, gradually reinforcing the idea of Tennessee whiskey as distinct from bourbon.

Recognizing this historical overlap is crucial when exploring cigar-and-whiskey rituals of the 1800s. In an era when consumers asked for "bourbon and a cigar," the bottle poured might have come from Kentucky, or just as likely, from a Tennessee distillery using the same practices. Only with time, branding, and law did the categories diverge.

Today, the legacy of blurred whiskey boundaries continues. While Tennessee whiskey is legally distinct, several Tennessee distilleries proudly use the word bourbon on their labels, acknowledging shared production standards and embracing the broader American whiskey tradition. Notable examples include:

- **Nelson's Green Brier Distillery**: Their flagship *Tennessee Whiskey* appears alongside *Tennessee Bourbon* bottlings.
- **Davidson Reserve**: Offers a *Tennessee Straight Bourbon Whiskey* aged and bottled in Nashville.
- **Chattanooga Whiskey Co.**: Markets products like *Chattanooga Whiskey 91*, labeled as *Tennessee High Malt Bourbon*.
- **J.W. Kelly & Co.**: Revived label includes *Old Milford Straight Bourbon Whiskey*, echoing its 19th-century roots.

**J.W. Kelly's Deep Spring Sour Mash Whiskey**—*distilled in Chattanooga beginning in 1866—illustrates how Tennessee whiskeys of the late 19th century were often indistinguishable in style and labeling from Kentucky bourbons. With charred oak aging and sour mash fermentation, products like Deep Spring were commonly marketed and grouped under the broader category of "fine bourbons."*

# Conclusion: The Height of Prestige and Transition to Modernity

The 19th century marked the apex of cultural prestige for bourbon and cigars in the United States. What began as regional specializations matured into national emblems of refinement, craftsmanship, and American identity. This transformation was propelled by expanding trade networks, industrial innovation, and strategic branding that elevated these goods beyond mere commodities into symbols of taste, leisure, and status.

Bourbon, with its bold profile and regional distinctiveness, had firmly established itself as the nation's defining spirit. Its appeal lay in a careful alchemy of grain selection, charred oak aging, and limestone-filtered water: factors that embodied both American ingenuity and geographic specificity. Likewise, cigar manufacturing, whether drawing on prized Cuban imports or premium American-grown tobacco, became synonymous with luxury, discipline, and social standing.

The pairing of bourbon and cigars became a ritualized expression of authority, discernment, and cultural fluency. From private clubs and boardrooms to literary salons and political gatherings, these products shaped the textures of American public and private life. Their convergence offered a shared language of indulgence, one that crossed regional and class lines while reflecting deeper values: patience, tradition, and refinement.

The Golden Age was ending. But the values it embodied — craft, ritual, identity — would endure. Figures like J.W. Kelly, who embodied the dual trades of tobacconist and distiller, serve as reminders that this pairing was not just sensory. It was structural.

# CHAPTER 3

# Prohibition & Post-War Decline (1920s–1960s)

The decades spanning the 1920s to the 1960s marked a dramatic reversal of fortune for both bourbon and cigars. Prohibition, the Great Depression, and the disruptions of World War II dismantled the momentum these industries had built during the 19th century. In the postwar years, consumer tastes shifted toward mass-produced goods, cigarettes, and clear spirits, leaving traditional bourbon and cigars behind in a rapidly modernizing marketplace.

Yet even during this period of decline, seeds of revival were quietly planted, setting the stage for a dramatic resurgence decades later.

## I. The Dark Days of Prohibition

The Prohibition[8] era—triggered by the ratification of the Eighteenth

---

[8] **Prohibition in the United States (1920–1933)** was a nationwide constitutional ban on the production, importation, transportation, and sale of alcoholic beverages. Enacted by the Eighteenth Amendment and enforced by the Volstead Act, Prohibition sought to eliminate alcohol-related crime and social problems. However, the policy instead led to a booming underground economy, the proliferation of speakeasies, and widespread corruption among law enforcement officials. The eventual repeal of Prohibition with the Twenty-first Amendment in 1933. was largely driven by public disillusionment with the policy's unintended consequences and the economic needs of the Great Depression.

Amendment in 1919 and enforced through the Volstead Act[9]—ushered in one of the most disruptive chapters in bourbon's history. What began as a national effort to eradicate alcohol swiftly dismantled an entire industry. Distilleries shuttered, jobs vanished, and a once-celebrated American spirit was driven underground.

For Kentucky, the consequences were especially severe. Generational distilleries closed overnight, leaving skilled workers idle and aging stock stranded in warehouses. The Volstead Act criminalized the manufacture, sale, and transport of intoxicating liquors, forcing bourbon into the shadows. While a few producers secured licenses for medicinal whiskey— exploiting a narrow legal loophole—most relied on secrecy or saw their operations collapse entirely. The era reshaped bourbon's image, linking it not with craftsmanship and tradition, but with bootlegging, black markets, and cultural resilience.

Yet, not all production ceased. A crucial loophole within the legislation allowed for the continued manufacture of whiskey for medicinal purposes.[10] Under this exemption, select distilleries were permitted to produce "medicinal bourbon," which could be legally sold through licensed pharmacies. Brands such as Old Forester and Four Roses, among the six federally licensed distillers, took advantage of this opportunity, marketing their products as legitimate medicinal remedies. During Prohibition, millions of prescriptions for medicinal whiskey were written each year, providing a lifeline for distilleries able to secure such licenses.

---

[9] **The Volstead Act**, officially known as the National Prohibition Act, was passed by Congress on October 28, 1919, to provide enforcement measures for the Eighteenth Amendment, which prohibited the manufacture, sale, and transportation of intoxicating liquors in the United States. Named after its sponsor, Congressman Andrew Volstead, the Act defined intoxicating liquor as any beverage containing more than 0.5% alcohol by volume.

[10] During Prohibition, whiskey was designated as a medicinal substance under Section 6 of the Volstead Act, allowing physicians to prescribe it and pharmacists to dispense it legally. While some doctors believed whiskey could ease symptoms such as colds, coughs, or anxiety, the majority of prescriptions were not grounded in rigorous medical evidence. Instead, this exemption became a widely exploited legal loophole. By some estimates, over 6 million whiskey prescriptions were issued annually at the height of Prohibition, with many consumers seeking treatment more for convenience than necessity. See: Lerner, Michael A. *Dry Manhattan: Prohibition in New York City* (Harvard University Press, 2007), 112–115.

Despite this legal avenue, the bourbon industry's scale and prestige were severely diminished. Brands that had once thrived now faced the harsh reality of limited production, distribution, and public perception. Meanwhile, countless smaller producers and independent distillers disappeared entirely, unable to adapt to the constraints of the new legal environment.

## The Rise of Bootlegging and Moonshine

While some distilleries survived under the guise of medicinal whiskey production, much of the bourbon market was overtaken by the black market. Prohibition inadvertently created fertile ground for bootlegging, a shadow industry that catered to America's undiminished thirst for whiskey and other spirits.

Bootleggers quickly capitalized on the demand for bourbon, establishing extensive underground networks to distribute illicit alcohol. Speakeasies—hidden, unlicensed establishments serving alcohol—proliferated across the country, particularly in urban centers like Chicago, New York, and New Orleans. Bourbon, once an emblem of American craftsmanship, became entangled with criminal enterprise and political corruption.

The underground market did not solely supply quality bourbon. Due to the high demand and low supply, many bootleggers resorted to producing inferior products known as "moonshine" or "rotgut." These unregulated spirits were often made hastily and with poor-quality ingredients, resulting in dangerous or even lethal concoctions. As the reputation of bourbon suffered, so too did the broader whiskey industry's standing in American culture.

The cultural impact of Prohibition on bourbon's image was profound. Rather than being celebrated as a symbol of craftsmanship and regional pride, bourbon became synonymous with criminality and recklessness.

This era would leave lasting scars on the industry, challenging distillers to rehabilitate bourbon's reputation once Prohibition was finally repealed.

However, even as Prohibition neared its end in 1933, bourbon faced another significant challenge: the economic devastation of the Great Depression.[11] With the bourbon market severely weakened, the Great Depression further exacerbated the decline of both bourbon and cigars. The cultural status and commercial viability of these products were increasingly threatened, forcing producers to adapt or risk complete collapse.

The next section explores how the cigar industry, facing its own existential crisis, attempted to navigate the harsh realities of economic collapse, shifting consumer preferences, and the rise of mechanized production.

## II. The Great Depression's Impact on American Cigar Production

The Great Depression compounded the damage already inflicted by Prohibition. For the cigar industry, which relied on discretionary spending, the crash brought immediate and widespread devastation.

### Economic Collapse and Its Effect on Luxury Goods

The widespread unemployment and financial instability caused by the Great Depression drastically altered consumer behavior. As millions of Americans lost their jobs and struggled to meet basic needs, the market for luxury items like premium cigars all but collapsed. The financial hardship

---

[11] **The Great Depression (1929–1939)** was the most severe economic downturn in American history, triggered by the stock market crash of October 1929. Its effects were devastating, with unemployment reaching approximately 25% and industrial production falling by nearly 50%. During this period, consumer spending sharply declined, forcing numerous businesses, including bourbon distilleries and cigar manufacturers, to close or drastically reduce their operations. The economic hardship intensified the challenges already faced by the bourbon and cigar industries due to Prohibition, making recovery particularly difficult.

of the era forced many to forgo their previously cherished indulgences, opting instead for more affordable alternatives or abandoning the habit altogether.

The repercussions were felt most acutely by the producers of high-quality cigars, particularly those reliant on hand-rolled techniques using premium tobacco. With consumers prioritizing necessities over luxury goods, cigar lounges and high-end tobacco shops saw their clientele diminish rapidly. Even the prominent Connecticut Broadleaf tobacco, once a staple of premium American cigars, struggled to find buyers.

As the economic downturn continued, cigar makers were forced to confront the harsh reality that the market for their traditional, high-quality products was rapidly shrinking. Something had to change if the industry was to survive.

The cigar industry adapted by embracing technological innovation and mass production methods.

## III. Machine-Made Cigars and the Decline of Tradition

Facing persistent financial instability and shrinking demand, cigar manufacturers increasingly relied on technological advancements to reduce costs and sustain production. This shift towards mechanization marked a turning point that would alter the cigar industry's landscape for decades to come.[12]

### Technological Advancements in Cigar Production

The introduction of cigar-rolling machines during the early 20th century provided a lifeline to manufacturers struggling to stay afloat. These

---

[12] The cigar industry reached its peak in the 1920s, with over 200 major factories producing approximately 500 million cigars in 1929 alone. However, the Great Depression marked the beginning of a significant decline in the industry. (Production figures from Museum of Florida History, "Cigar Box Labels Collection.")

machines, designed to replace the intricate work of human hands, could produce cigars at a rate previously unimaginable. By the 1930s, as the economic hardships of the Great Depression persisted, mechanized production became the dominant mode of manufacturing for most companies.

The economic benefits of mechanization were undeniable. Factories could now produce cigars at a fraction of the previous cost, allowing companies to sell their products at prices affordable to even the most financially strained consumers. In an era when luxury goods were increasingly seen as frivolous, this shift was essential for maintaining any semblance of profitability.

However, the move towards industrialized cigar production came with significant drawbacks. The mass-production methods favored speed and efficiency over quality and craftsmanship. Unlike hand-rolled cigars, which required meticulous attention to detail and skillful blending of tobacco leaves, machine-made cigars relied on homogenized filler, lower-grade tobacco, and artificial flavoring to maintain consistency and reduce costs.

The widespread adoption of these techniques drastically altered the public perception of cigars. No longer exclusively associated with luxury, refinement, and ritual, cigars became increasingly viewed as everyday, disposable products. This fundamental shift in perception would haunt the industry for decades, as the prestige of the hand-rolled cigar gave way to the commercial success of its mass-produced counterpart.[13]

---

[13] The mechanization of cigar production in the early 20th century significantly transformed the industry. Between 1921 and 1936, the number of U.S. cigar manufacturing establishments declined from 14,578 to 5,292. In that same period, the number of factories producing 40 million or more cigars annually rose from 11 to 27, increasing their share of total output from 15.7% to 56.5%. Meanwhile, the proportion of cigars retailing at 5 cents or less surged from 30% to 88%—a reflection of how mechanization and price competition reshaped the industry.[1] These shifts disproportionately harmed small, family-run shops, many of which failed during the Depression or were absorbed by larger mechanized firms. See Pamela K. Laird, *"Pull: Networking and Success Since Benjamin Franklin"* (Cambridge, MA: Harvard University Press, 2006), 217-218.

Mechanization helped many companies stay afloat but compromised the cigar industry's core identity. In response, a growing niche began to revalue craftsmanship, signaling early resistance to homogenized production.

## Artisanal Producers vs. Corporate Giants

For generations, hand-rolled cigars were revered as an art form, an intergenerational craft rooted in patience, precision, and pride. But by the mid-20th century, that tradition was under siege.

As corporate manufacturers embraced mechanization to produce cigars at scale, smaller producers found themselves at a disadvantage. Without the capital to invest in machinery or the marketing muscle to compete nationally, many artisanal makers either shuttered or were forced to compromise their standards to survive.

This growing divide between craftsmanship and industrialization came to define the cigar industry during this period. Mass-produced cigars flooded the market, redefining public perception. What was once a symbol of luxury and leisure risked becoming a disposable, commodified good. Yet a small but steadfast cohort of artisans held firm, preserving traditional rolling techniques and resisting the tide of homogenization.

---

## Survivors and Consolidators — How Cigar Brands Navigated the Industrial Shift

The era of mechanization and corporate consolidation in the cigar industry (1920s–1960s) forced manufacturers into a stark choice: adapt, vanish, or be acquired. Some brands preserved their artisanal heritage through resilience and innovation. Others were absorbed by larger conglomerates, often losing their identity in the process. Together, they reflect the industry's complex transition from craftsmanship to commodification.

**Brands That Survived While Preserving Craftsmanship**

- **Arturo Fuente (est. 1912)**: Founded in West Tampa, FL, Fuente rebuilt after a devastating 1924 fire and resumed production in 1946. Over the decades, it became a standard-bearer of hand-rolled excellence, later relocating to the Dominican Republic.
- **J.C. Newman (est. 1895)**: One of the few family-owned U.S. cigar companies to survive the Great Depression and industrial pressures. It blended mechanization with premium production and remains operational today in Tampa's historic El Reloj factory.

**Brands That Were Acquired and Industrialized**

- **Macanudo**: Originally a small Cuban brand, it was revived and reblended by General Cigar in the 1970s. It became one of the first machine-made cigars marketed as "premium," signaling a new hybrid approach to tradition and scale.
- **Muriel Cigars (est. 1912)**: Known for affordability and machine production, Muriel was eventually acquired by Lorillard and later became part of Altadis USA—an emblem of the consolidation trend that reshaped mid-century cigar culture.

These brand trajectories reveal the industry's bifurcation: a mainstream market shaped by efficiency and volume, and a niche countercurrent determined to preserve legacy and labor-intensive artistry.

---

At the same time, corporate consolidation became a common trend. Larger companies acquired smaller producers, sometimes preserving their brand names but drastically altering the quality and process of production. This shift not only affected the physical product but also the cultural symbolism of cigars. What had once been a luxury item representing sophistication and leisure was now increasingly viewed as a cheap, mass-market commodity.

Yet, within this period of decline, the seeds of revival were being planted. As the corporate giants continued to prioritize efficiency over quality, a small but growing counterculture emerged, one that championed individuality, legacy, and a slower, more intentional approach to production. This movement would not gain widespread traction until decades later, but it represented a critical undercurrent of resistance against the homogenization of the industry.

## IV. Bourbon's Decline in the Age of Vodka and Scotch

Having barely survived Prohibition, bourbon faced new threats in the mid-20th century: changing tastes, global competition, and the rise of corporate conglomerates. As a new generation of drinkers gravitated toward lighter spirits—vodka and blended Scotch—bourbon's traditional appeal struggled to keep pace.

### Post-Prohibition Struggles

The repeal of Prohibition in 1933 was greeted with jubilation by bourbon producers, but the aftermath proved to be far more challenging than anticipated. Nearly fourteen years of restricted production had devastated the industry's infrastructure. Distilleries that had been shuttered during Prohibition required extensive repairs or complete rebuilding. Moreover, skilled laborers who had left the industry to pursue other professions were difficult to replace, and many distilleries simply lacked the financial resources to restart operations.

To complicate matters, the American public's relationship with bourbon had fundamentally changed. The forced cessation of legal production had altered cultural habits and created a void that other spirits eagerly filled. Although medicinal whiskey production continued during Prohibition, much of the bourbon consumed during this period was of poor quality, produced by illicit bootleggers with little regard for craftsmanship or safety. The public's distrust of whiskey products was not easily overcome.

Additionally, the economic devastation of the Great Depression lingered well into the late 1930s, reducing the disposable income available for luxury goods like premium bourbon. Even when production resumed, distillers faced an uphill battle to convince consumers that their products were worth the investment.

These struggles were further compounded by the impact of World War II, which diverted resources away from bourbon production and altered public preferences in ways that would have long-lasting consequences.

## Wartime Production and Market Displacement

The advent of World War II proved to be another formidable challenge for the bourbon industry. As the United States mobilized for war, the federal government imposed strict rationing on essential materials, including grains used in bourbon production. Distilleries across the country were either shut down or repurposed to produce industrial-grade alcohol necessary for the war effort, including solvents and medicinal alcohol.

During this period, bourbon production plummeted. Brands that managed to survive did so largely by producing what little they could under government regulations. But the lack of consistency and availability during the war years only further weakened bourbon's market position.

Furthermore, the war effort had profound cultural effects. Soldiers stationed abroad were introduced to a variety of foreign spirits, particularly Scotch whisky, which would later play a significant role in transforming American drinking preferences. Blended Scotch, with its smoother, milder profile, appealed to a broader demographic than the robust, often harsh qualities of bourbon.

The postwar economic boom of the 1950s also contributed to bourbon's decline. As Americans enjoyed unprecedented prosperity, their tastes shifted toward what was perceived as more sophisticated, cosmopolitan spirits. Vodka, which was marketed as clean, modern, and versatile, quickly became the drink of choice for a new generation.

As bourbon producers scrambled to regain their footing, a new era of corporate consolidation and aggressive marketing would only intensify the competition, pushing bourbon further into the background of American drinking culture.

## The Rise of Vodka and Scotch

For consumers who had grown up during the war years, bourbon represented an outdated relic of a previous generation. They sought beverages that were lighter, cleaner, and more versatile, attributes that vodka marketers emphasized relentlessly.

The rise of vodka was propelled by savvy advertising campaigns that promoted its neutrality and mixability. By framing vodka as a sophisticated and modern alternative, marketers were able to attract young, upwardly mobile consumers eager to distinguish themselves from their parents' generation. Cocktail culture flourished, with vodka-based drinks like the Moscow Mule, Screwdriver, and Bloody Mary becoming staples of fashionable social life.

Blended Scotch also emerged as a popular choice, benefiting from both its association with British refinement and its palatable flavor profile. Unlike bourbon's bold and sometimes abrasive character, blended Scotch was often described as smooth and approachable, qualities that resonated with a public increasingly enamored with international sophistication.

At the same time, large liquor conglomerates expanded their portfolios and aggressively promoted their global brands. While bourbon producers clung to heritage and craftsmanship, Scotch and vodka companies embraced modernity, innovation, and mass appeal. The effect was a dramatic shift in the liquor market that left bourbon struggling to compete.

By the end of the 1960s, bourbon's cultural relevance had significantly diminished. Its association with the past, combined with the dominance of vodka and Scotch, left it languishing as a niche product with declining prestige. The industry's decline was so severe that many smaller distilleries were forced to close their doors permanently.

## Conclusion: Decline, Survival, and the Fragile Flame of Tradition

The period from the 1920s to the 1960s was marked by relentless challenges for both the bourbon and cigar industries. Prohibition nearly dismantled bourbon production, reducing the field to a handful of licensed medicinal distillers. In parallel, the Great Depression and rapid mechanization forced the cigar industry into a period of compromise, with quality and craftsmanship sacrificed for survival.

In the postwar decades, cultural tastes shifted further away from tradition. Vodka and blended Scotch displaced bourbon on liquor shelves, while cigarettes and machine-made cigars overtook their handcrafted predecessors. By the end of the 1960s, both industries had lost their once-prized status, becoming relics of a bygone era in the eyes of a modernizing public.

Yet beneath the surface, pockets of resistance persisted. A few distillers, rollers, and tobacco growers refused to abandon their crafts, preserving knowledge and methods that would one day prove vital. Though marginalized and largely invisible, these traditions endured—fragile, but unextinguished.

In the next chapter, we turn to the global disruptions and regional adaptations that forced the cigar and bourbon industries to rethink everything. From the sudden exile of Cuban cigars to bourbon's struggle for identity, this next phase set the stage not for nostalgia, but for reinvention.

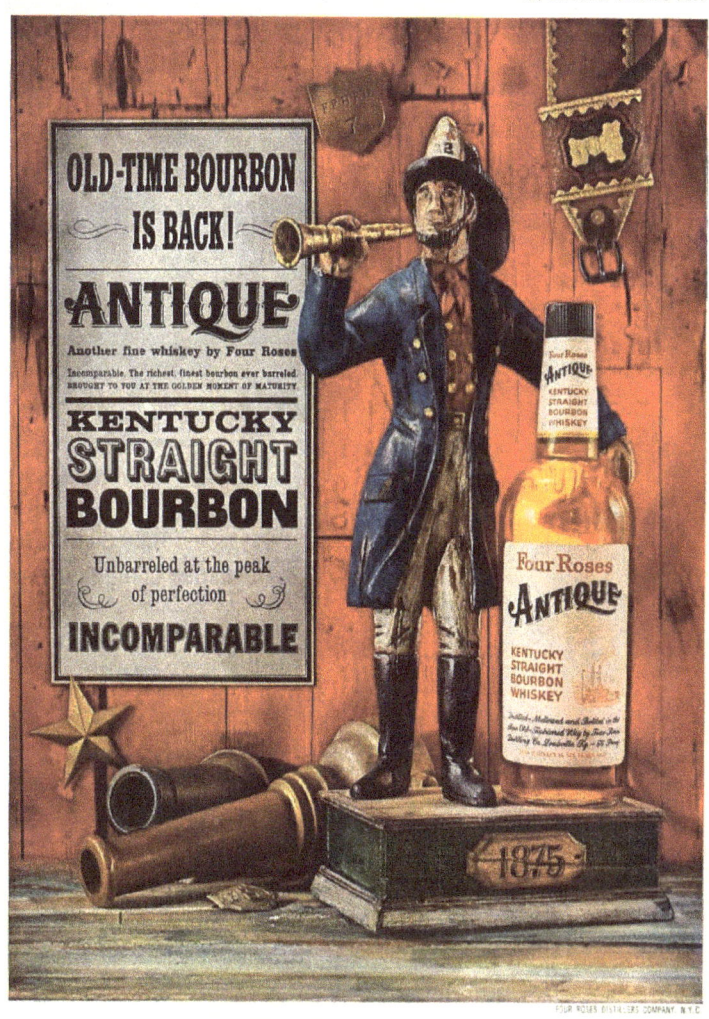

**"Old Time Bourbon Is Back!"**: *This 1959 Four Roses ad captures the postwar revival of heritage and craftsmanship in American bourbon—celebrating a return to antique Kentucky traditions in an age of modernity.*

# CHAPTER 4

# The Cuban Embargo &
# Industry Reinvention
# (1962–1990s)

The 1962 Cuban Embargo marked a watershed moment for the American cigar industry, abruptly severing access to Cuban tobacco, historically revered for its unparalleled quality. This sudden disruption forced manufacturers, consumers, and artisans alike to adapt swiftly, paving the way for an industry-wide transformation. Simultaneously, bourbon faced its own crisis: shifting consumer tastes, aggressive corporate consolidation, and intensified competition from lighter spirits pushed America's native whiskey into cultural and economic decline. This chapter examines how these parallel disruptions spurred remarkable innovations in cigar production and set the stage for bourbon's quiet resurgence. Driven by a renewed commitment to craftsmanship and authenticity, both industries ultimately reinvented themselves, laying the foundation for a cultural renaissance that would fully blossom in the decades to come.

# I. The Cuban Embargo: A Turning Point for Cigars

The early 1960s profoundly reshaped the cigar industry, marking a critical turning point. As Cold War tensions between the United States and the Soviet Union intensified—particularly after Cuba aligned itself with the Soviet bloc—President John F. Kennedy signed Proclamation 3447 on February 3, 1962, initiating a full trade embargo against Cuba.[14] The embargo banned all imports from the island, including its world-renowned cigars.

For decades, Cuban cigars had been regarded as the gold standard, celebrated for their rich flavor profiles, exquisite craftsmanship, and the unique qualities derived from tobacco grown in Cuba's fertile Vuelta Abajo region. The sudden disappearance of Cuban cigars from the American market was not only a shock to consumers but also a challenge to the industry itself. The embargo forced both producers and consumers to adapt, setting off a chain reaction that would reshape the cigar market for generations.

## The Embargo's Immediate Impact

The 1962 embargo marked a pivotal rupture in the U.S. cigar market, where Cuban cigars had long reigned as the pinnacle of quality and prestige. Their abrupt disappearance left a vacuum that sparked a wave of both imitation and innovation across the global cigar landscape.

American consumers, accustomed to the rich, complex flavors of Cuban cigars, were left searching for suitable replacements. Initially, demand

---

[14] On February 3, 1962, President John F. Kennedy signed Proclamation 3447, initiating a full trade embargo against Cuba. Issued under the authority of the Foreign Assistance Act and the Trading With the Enemy Act, the order prohibited "all imports of goods of Cuban origin into the United States", including Cuba's famed cigars and rum. The proclamation went into effect on February 7, 1962, just days after being signed. While framed as part of broader Cold War efforts to economically isolate Fidel Castro's communist regime, its impact on consumer culture was profound and enduring. For American cigar smokers, it meant the immediate and indefinite disappearance of the world's most coveted cigars from store shelves.

outstripped supply, and many consumers turned to contraband Cuban cigars smuggled through Canada or Mexico. Others reluctantly switched to lower-quality cigars made domestically or imported from other nations with less developed cigar industries.

The embargo was intended as a political tool to isolate Cuba economically, but its unintended consequence was the forced diversification of the global cigar industry. Without access to Cuban tobacco, American manufacturers and distributors were compelled to look elsewhere to satisfy consumer demand. This disruption of established trade patterns would prove to be both a challenge and an opportunity, as new regions and manufacturers sought to fill the void left by Cuba's exclusion from the American market.

## The Rise of New Cigar Regions

While the embargo initially created a crisis for the American cigar industry, it also catalyzed the rise of new production centers across the Caribbean and Central America. Central to this rapid emergence was the relocation of skilled Cuban artisans, whose expertise played a pivotal role in establishing thriving cigar industries outside of Cuba.

The Dominican Republic was the first to benefit from this migration. The country's fertile soil and favorable climate proved to be well-suited for tobacco cultivation, and soon exiled Cuban cigar makers were establishing farms, factories, and brands that would eventually rival their Cuban predecessors. Notable among these was Arturo Fuente, a brand that would go on to become synonymous with premium cigar craftsmanship.

Nicaragua and Honduras also emerged as significant players, thanks to similar geographical advantages and the expertise brought by Cuban émigrés. By the 1980s, brands like Padron and La Aurora were building reputations for excellence. Despite initial skepticism about whether these new regions could truly replicate the quality of Cuban cigars, they gradually carved out their own unique flavor profiles and identities.

The exiled Cuban artisans not only recreated what they had lost but also innovated. They experimented with new blends, aging processes, and curing techniques, developing a distinctive cigar culture separate from its Cuban roots.

U.S.-grown tobaccos—especially Connecticut Shade and Pennsylvania Broadleaf—offered complementary flavor profiles to Caribbean and Central American leaves. As exiled Cuban artisans blended regional tobaccos with premium American wrappers and binders, they helped establish a new generation of distinctive brands and flavor identities.

What emerged from this upheaval was a far more diverse and resilient cigar market. Cuban cigars continued to be prized around the world, but their absence from the U.S. market allowed alternative producers to develop their own reputations.

## II. Rebuilding the Cigar Industry

Cigar makers who relocated to the Dominican Republic, Nicaragua, and Honduras faced daunting challenges: unfamiliar soils, different climates, and a skeptical market accustomed to Cuban cigars as the gold standard. Cuba's ideal growing conditions were no longer available — they had to be approximated, adapted, or replaced.

Yet necessity spurred creativity. Traditional techniques were modified, hybrid seeds were cultivated, and local terroirs were embraced rather than resisted. The goal was not simply to imitate what was lost, but to craft something new—flavor profiles that honored the past while reflecting their new environments, marrying craftsmanship with regional distinctiveness.

### The Role of American-Grown Tobacco

As the global cigar map shifted, American growers also played a key role in sustaining and redefining the industry. The Connecticut River Valley became a vital partner in the post-embargo transformation. Its two signature varietals—Connecticut Shade and Connecticut Broadleaf—offered unique qualities that helped replace the complex flavor contributions of Cuban tobacco.

Shade-grown wrappers provided elegance and smoothness, while Broadleaf added strength, sweetness, and a rich, earthy depth. These American leaves became integral to new blends that appealed to evolving consumer palates, especially in Maduro and premium hand-rolled cigars. By the late 1980s, these tobaccos were no longer substitutes; they were assets in their own right, featured proudly in celebrated lines like Fuente's Hemingway and Padron's Anniversary series.

### Toward a New Premium Standard

This period of reinvention laid the foundation for what would become the Cigar Renaissance of the 1990s. Far from a retreat, the cigar industry's response to the embargo was a pivot: away from singular dependence on Cuban terroir and toward a diverse ecosystem of quality-driven production rooted in global expertise and local innovation.

It was not only about survival. It was about setting a new standard. As the next chapter will show, this quiet rebuilding would soon give way to explosive growth, fueled by media, celebrity culture, and a renewed consumer appetite for authenticity.

## III. Bourbon's Identity Crisis: From the 1960s to the 1990s

While the cigar industry responded to the Cuban embargo with adaptation and innovation, bourbon faced its own slow-burning identity crisis. From the 1960s through the 1990s, a convergence of cultural, economic, and industrial pressures pushed America's native spirit into a deep decline. The rise of lighter liquors, aggressive corporate consolidation, and a growing disconnect between producers and tradition eroded bourbon's reputation and consumer base. Yet, beneath the surface, the values of craftsmanship and authenticity endured, and would eventually power bourbon's return.

## Changing Tastes and Declining Prestige

By the 1960s, the American palate was shifting. Vodka, gin, and blended Scotch gained popularity for their light, mixable qualities, increasingly associated with modern sophistication and cosmopolitan culture. Vodka was sold as odorless and tasteless—a blank canvas for the booming cocktail scene. Blended Scotch was marketed as the refined alternative to bourbon, which now seemed too rough, too Southern, too old-fashioned for postwar sensibilities.

Hollywood glamorized the martini; advertising campaigns for imported spirits cast bourbon as outdated. Younger drinkers gravitated toward international flavors, and bourbon became more closely associated with older, working-class consumers. By the 1970s and 1980s, it had lost its place as a national symbol of refinement and innovation, slipping instead into obscurity.

## Corporate Consolidation and the Loss of Craft

At the same time, economic pressures reshaped the bourbon industry from within. Large conglomerates—such as National Distillers, Schenley Industries, and later Seagram and Brown-Forman—acquired historic bourbon brands and prioritized volume over quality. Aging times were reduced. Barrel rotation practices were abandoned. Mash bills were altered for cost efficiency. Once-distinctive flavor profiles were flattened in the name of consistency.

---

### Turning the Barrel — Kentucky and Tennessee Rotate Their Whiskey

Barrel rotation is a uniquely American aging practice most closely associated with traditional bourbon and Tennessee whiskey production. In both Kentucky and Tennessee, distillers often age their spirits in tall, multi-story rickhouses where dramatic temperature differences between floors can significantly impact flavor and maturation rates.

In these non-climate-controlled warehouses, barrels stored on upper levels experience hotter temperatures and faster aging, while those on lower floors age more slowly and develop different flavor profiles. To even out these effects and ensure a more balanced final product, some distilleries manually rotate barrels—moving them from floor to floor over time.

This labor-intensive practice is most closely associated with Kentucky and Tennessee, though some craft producers in other regions have adopted similar approaches. In contrast, distilleries in Scotland, Ireland, and many newer whiskey regions often use low, climate-stable warehouses that eliminate the need for rotation. The tradition in the American South, however, reflects a distinctive commitment to environmental interaction and flavor consistency.

While not all Kentucky and Tennessee distilleries rotate barrels today—some rely on blending to achieve uniformity—the practice remains a hallmark of hands-on bourbon and Tennessee whiskey craftsmanship.

---

This shift toward industrial-scale production marked a sharp departure from bourbon's roots. Traditional, regional identities were subsumed into generic branding. Small, family-run distilleries were shuttered or absorbed. The unique craftsmanship that had once defined the industry was sacrificed for corporate streamlining. During this period of corporate takeover, bourbon as a regional craft was nearly lost.

By the mid-1980s, bourbon had reached a nadir. Sales stagnated. Prestige evaporated. Scotch was booming; in America, vodka reigned. Many bourbon brands survived only by cutting costs and relying on a dwindling loyal customer base. It seemed plausible that bourbon might become a relic of the past.

## Quiet Resistance and Cultural Undercurrents

Yet even during this bleak era, a few producers and enthusiasts quietly resisted the tide of homogenization. Some distilleries continued to make bourbon the old way, not because it was profitable but because it was right. Brands like Maker's Mark, which eschewed corporate efficiency in favor of hand-dipped bottles and wheated mash bills, offered a glimmer of authenticity. So did private collectors, bourbon historians, and small-scale bottlers who preserved knowledge, tradition, and pride.

These pockets of resistance in the bourbon world paralleled the quiet reinvention taking place in the cigar world. The seeds of revival were planted. What remained was the right moment, and the right audience, to bring bourbon back to life.

## IV. The Seeds of Revival: Bourbon, Cigars, and the Return to Craft

As the 20th century drew to a close, the bourbon and cigar industries, once dismissed as outdated relics, began to show signs of an unexpected transformation. What emerged was not yet a full-scale boom—that would come in the 1990s—but a growing undercurrent of revival powered by artisans, entrepreneurs, and enthusiasts determined to reclaim authenticity, heritage, and quality.

In bourbon, this renewal began quietly. A few visionary distillers rejected the industry's race to the bottom and returned to time-honored methods: longer aging periods, single-barrel expressions, and wheated mash bills (using wheat as the secondary grain instead of rye) that prioritized complexity over volume. Their commitment to tradition—often against prevailing corporate logic—reintroduced bourbon as a craft worth preserving. The quiet reappearance of smooth, amber spirits on specialty shelves marked a departure from the harsh, mass-market labels of previous decades.

Cigars, too, were stirring. While still burdened by the aftershocks of the Cuban embargo and waning cultural relevance, non-Cuban cigar makers had begun to refine their craft. Producers in the Dominican Republic, Nicaragua, and Honduras—many founded by Cuban expatriates—were experimenting with fermentation, rolling techniques, and wrapper varietals. Their efforts were laying the groundwork for a premium cigar market that could stand on its own, not as a substitute for Cuban tobacco, but as a legitimate evolution of it.

These parallel movements reflected a deeper cultural shift. In an era increasingly saturated with mass production and synthetic uniformity, consumers were beginning to crave experiences rooted in craftsmanship and story. For bourbon and cigars alike, this meant rediscovering their historical identities—not as symbols of excess or nostalgia, but as artisanal expressions of labor, land, and legacy.

This transitional period was not yet a renaissance, but it was the spark. It redefined the possibility of what bourbon and cigars could become—not just again, but anew. It set the stage for a cultural resurgence that would soon bring both industries back to the forefront of American taste and identity.

## Conclusion: Revival Before Renaissance

By the end of the 1980s, both the cigar and bourbon industries had endured profound transformation. What began as forced adaptation—triggered by geopolitical rupture for cigars and cultural decline for bourbon—evolved into something more enduring: a slow, deliberate return to craft. Disruption had not destroyed these industries; it had forced them to rediscover their roots.

In the wake of the Cuban embargo, exiled cigar makers helped establish new centers of excellence across the Caribbean and Central America, blending traditional knowledge with innovative methods. Meanwhile, a handful of bourbon distillers quietly resisted homogenization, choosing to refine aging techniques, embrace small-batch production, and protect the integrity of their craft.

These parallel recoveries were not yet revolutions. But they represented a powerful reorientation, away from commodification and toward authenticity. The values of heritage, quality, and regional identity had begun to reassert themselves, laying the groundwork for what would soon become a cultural and economic renaissance.

These early signals of revival would soon gain momentum. In the 1990s, a perfect storm of cultural appetite, strategic marketing, and renewed connoisseurship would bring bourbon and cigars roaring back into American life—not merely as luxuries, but as symbols of craftsmanship, connection, and tradition reimagined.

# CHAPTER 5

# The Renaissance

*The 1990s Boom in Cigars & Bourbon*

The 1990s ignited a full-scale renaissance for cigars and bourbon, industries that had quietly rebuilt themselves over the previous decades and were now ready to reclaim the cultural spotlight. No longer relics of a bygone era, they surged into relevance, reshaped by a confluence of media influence, deliberate marketing, and a renewed public hunger for authenticity.

Cigars reemerged as potent symbols of status and celebration, fueled by the so-called "Cigar Boom," which transformed them into lifestyle accessories for a new generation of professionals and tastemakers. Meanwhile, bourbon—once dismissed as antiquated—was rediscovered through small-batch expressions and heritage branding that elevated it to a staple of refined American taste.

This chapter explores how a perfect storm of cultural appetite, artisanal innovation, and media amplification turned cigars and bourbon into complementary icons of sophistication, forging a new era of connoisseurship rooted in tradition, storytelling, and sensory pleasure.

# I. The Cigar Boom: A New Era of Appreciation

The resurgence of cigars was not a random occurrence but rather the result of strategic marketing efforts, shifts in popular culture, and the emergence of new and sophisticated cigar production techniques that had developed over the previous decades.

One of the most significant contributors to the revival was the launch of *Cigar Aficionado* magazine in 1992. Founded by Marvin Shanken, the glossy publication was the first of its kind to frame cigars as part of a broader lifestyle of affluence, leisure, and discerning taste. Its pages featured glamorous photo spreads of celebrities such as Arnold Schwarzenegger, Michael Jordan, and Jack Nicholson, all of whom were avid cigar enthusiasts. By associating cigars with powerful, successful men, *Cigar Aficionado* played a central role in reshaping public perceptions of cigar smoking.

Moreover, the magazine featured articles that went beyond product reviews, delving into the art and craft of cigar making, the historical significance of cigar culture, and the social rituals associated with smoking. This newfound media attention encouraged enthusiasts to view cigar smoking as more than just a habit; it was a refined experience that demanded appreciation and understanding.

As demand for premium cigars skyrocketed, producers across the Caribbean Basin rose to meet the challenge. The cigar diaspora from the Cuban Embargo had fully matured by the 1990s into thriving industries in the Dominican Republic, Nicaragua, and Honduras. Davidoff joined prominent brands like Arturo Fuente and Padron, whose meticulous craftsmanship and innovative blends became internationally acclaimed. Fuente's Opus X line, launched in 1995, quickly became one of the world's most coveted cigars, praised for its rich, complex flavor.

**Jack Nicholson Summer 1995** – *Jack Nicholson graces the summer 1995 cover of Cigar Aficionado, symbolizing the cigar boom's cultural peak as Hollywood icons embraced cigars as markers of power, style, and refined rebellion.*

Nicaragua and Honduras also rose to prominence during this period. Padron, a Nicaraguan brand known for its Maduro-wrapped cigars, became synonymous with quality and consistency. Meanwhile, Honduras established itself as a reliable producer of high-quality, robust cigars that competed effectively on the global stage.

While Cuban cigars retained their mystique, the embargo-driven innovation in places like Nicaragua, the Dominican Republic, and Honduras gave rise to a new generation of premium cigars, defined not by replication but by experimentation and adaptation.

American-grown Connecticut Shade and Broadleaf tobaccos remained central to modern premium cigar craftsmanship, offering a range from refined mildness to bold complexity for a new generation of enthusiasts.

What truly made the Cigar Boom of the 1990s remarkable was how it bridged the gap between old-world craftsmanship and modern marketing techniques. Producers embraced transparency in their manufacturing processes, highlighting the origins of their tobaccos, the aging techniques they employed, and the artisanal skills involved in rolling each cigar by hand.

The profound impact of the Cigar Boom was not only cultural but also economic. The sudden spike in demand encouraged further investments in production, quality control, and marketing. The revival of the cigar industry was a testament to the resilience of cigar makers who, despite political and economic setbacks, found new ways to flourish.

This renewed interest in cigars also established the foundation for a larger cultural phenomenon: the refined pairing of cigars with premium spirits, particularly bourbon. The growing appreciation for high-quality cigars would soon be matched by an equally passionate rediscovery of bourbon's craftsmanship and complexity. The stage was now set for the bourbon revival that would parallel the cigar boom in its scope and intensity.

## II. The Bourbon Revival: From Bottom Shelf to Top Shelf

The bourbon industry had spent the latter half of the 20<sup>th</sup> century struggling to maintain relevance in a market dominated by lighter spirits such as vodka and gin. To many, bourbon was seen as a relic of the past, a harsh and unsophisticated drink better suited for rough-and-tumble frontier life than modern, cosmopolitan society. However, as with the cigar industry, a dedicated group of enthusiasts and visionaries would eventually reclaim bourbon's legacy by focusing on craftsmanship, authenticity, and innovation.

The seeds of bourbon's revival were planted by a handful of influential figures, like Julian Van Winkle III, Elmer T. Lee, and Booker Noe, who saw that the industry's decline reflected not changing tastes but a failure to maintain quality and tradition. Van Winkle, honoring his grandfather "Pappy" Van Winkle's legacy, boldly introduced Pappy Van Winkle's Family Reserve—an aged bourbon whose meticulous craftsmanship initially faced skepticism. However, once the market recognized its unique flavor profile—marked by rich, complex layers of caramel, vanilla, and spice—it quickly became one of the most sought-after and respected bourbons in the world.

Elmer T. Lee, a master distiller at Buffalo Trace, similarly contributed to the bourbon renaissance by introducing the first single-barrel bourbon, Blanton's, in 1984. Lee's emphasis on quality over mass production was a radical departure from industry norms at the time. By bottling bourbon from a single barrel rather than blending multiple barrels, he showcased the distinct flavor profiles that could be achieved through careful aging and selection.

Booker Noe, the grandson of Jim Beam, took a different but complementary approach. He introduced the concept of "small-batch" bourbon, producing limited quantities of high-quality whiskey that emphasized robust flavors and traditional distillation methods. His Booker's bourbon, an unfiltered, high-proof spirit, became a favorite among enthusiasts who appreciated its bold, uncompromising character.

**Pappy Van Winkle's Family Reserve 23-Year-Old (1998, Gold Wax, Green Glass, Lawrenceburg)** — *A legendary bottle from the heart of the bourbon renaissance, this rare release epitomizes the craftsmanship, heritage, and cult status that transformed Pappy into the ultimate symbol of premium American whiskey.*

These pioneers of bourbon revitalization were not merely reviving a product; they were reclaiming an art form. The processes they championed—longer aging periods, single-barrel bottlings, and small-batch production—represented a return to the craftsmanship and dedication that had originally made bourbon one of America's most iconic spirits.

The emphasis on quality was further bolstered by the rise of brands such as Buffalo Trace, Maker's Mark, and Woodford Reserve. Each of these distilleries approached the bourbon revival with a distinct strategy that underscored the movement's diversity and creativity.

Buffalo Trace, under the stewardship of Mark Brown and master distillers like Elmer T. Lee and Harlen Wheatley, committed itself to innovation while preserving traditional methods. Its experimental program, which included unique aging conditions and novel grain recipes, exemplified how the bourbon industry could honor its past while embracing the future.

Maker's Mark distinguished itself by promoting a softer, wheated bourbon that appealed to consumers who preferred a smoother, less assertive flavor profile. Its iconic red-wax seal became a hallmark of quality and craftsmanship, appealing to consumers who valued authenticity and heritage.

Woodford Reserve, revived by the Brown-Forman Corporation in the mid-1990s, emphasized its historical roots by reopening the historic Labrot & Graham distillery in Versailles, Kentucky. Marketing itself as a premium bourbon focused on craftsmanship, Woodford Reserve quickly established itself as a leader in the small-batch movement.

Bourbon's revival was rooted in substance rather than style. It was not about creating a fad; it was about restoring bourbon's reputation by delivering a superior product. The meticulous attention to detail, combined with marketing efforts that highlighted bourbon's history and authenticity, gradually won over both enthusiasts and casual drinkers alike.

Part of this revival also involved a shift in how bourbon was marketed and consumed. Rather than shying away from bourbon's historical associations with rustic Americana, distilleries embraced their heritage and turned it into a selling point. Bourbon tourism became a burgeoning industry, with distilleries across Kentucky investing in guided tours, tastings, and visitor centers designed to enhance the consumer experience.

The Bourbon Trail, established in 1999 by the Kentucky Distillers' Association,[15] played a pivotal role in promoting bourbon as a cultural artifact worth preserving. By inviting consumers to explore the history, craftsmanship, and artistry of bourbon-making, the trail reinforced bourbon's status as a uniquely American spirit.

The resurgence of bourbon was not merely an exercise in nostalgia. It was a deliberate effort to redefine what bourbon could be in the modern world. By the end of the 1990s, the movement had successfully shifted bourbon from the bottom shelf to the top shelf, with premium releases commanding respect and high prices.

Furthermore, the bourbon revival dovetailed perfectly with the contemporaneous cigar renaissance. As cigar lounges proliferated, curated bourbon pairings reinforced the sophistication and craftsmanship emblematic of both products, elevating their joint cultural prestige.

The pairing of cigars and bourbon became emblematic of a broader cultural trend that valued craftsmanship, heritage, and quality. Whether it was a Pappy Van Winkle Family Reserve bourbon or a Padrón 1964 Anniversary Series cigar, enthusiasts were willing to pay a premium for experiences that felt both authentic and luxurious.

---

[15] As of early 2025, the Kentucky Bourbon Trail® encompasses 60 destinations across 27 counties in Kentucky. This expansion includes both major distilleries and smaller craft operations, reflecting remarkable growth from the original seven distilleries that formed the trail in 1999. The Bourbon Trail has become a vital force in promoting bourbon as a cultural and economic asset, drawing millions of visitors annually and reinforcing Kentucky's identity as the heart of American whiskey production. For current details and participating distilleries.

The bourbon revival, like the Cigar Boom, was not a return to past glories but rather a reinvention that paid homage to tradition while embracing innovation. The resurgence of both industries demonstrated that cultural relevance and commercial success could be achieved not by abandoning history, but by drawing strength from it.

**Buffalo Trace Distillery** — Perched along the Kentucky River in Frankfort, the Buffalo Trace Distillery stands as the most visited bourbon distillery in the state—a living testament to the enduring legacy of American whiskey craftsmanship.

## III. Pop Culture's Role in the Renaissance

As bourbon and cigars gradually reclaimed their identities through craftsmanship and innovation, popular culture emerged as a powerful amplifier, catapulting both into the mainstream not through production methods, but through symbolism, lifestyle marketing, and mass media storytelling. The 1990s cultural landscape was primed for this shift. In an era increasingly skeptical of mass-produced goods and generic branding, consumers began to seek objects that connoted authenticity, tradition, and sensory richness. Bourbon and cigars, with their tactile rituals and deep historical roots, offered precisely that.

Cinema and television helped reshape public perception. Films like *Heat* (1995), *Casino* (1995), and the HBO series *The Sopranos* (1999) featured protagonists whose indulgence in cigars and whiskey signaled power, masculinity, and control. These weren't background props. They were visual metaphors for status and deliberation. On screen, the slow draw of a cigar or the deliberate pour of a bourbon became gestures that reinforced identity, taste, and authority.

At the same time, a growing number of lifestyle publications contributed to the resurgence. Most influential among them was *Cigar Aficionado*, which (as noted earlier) helped reframe cigar smoking as aspiration rather than habit.

Though *Cigar Aficionado* would later spotlight bourbon in its features—a development explored in the next section—its early issues established the template for repositioning once-declining traditions through the lens of lifestyle media. Other magazines soon followed suit, as did product placement deals, fashion spreads, and ad campaigns. Bourbon brands began emphasizing heritage and small-batch quality. Cigars became standard fare at high-end parties and luxury events. Both industries were reimagined as not just products, but experiences.

This cultural momentum had a cumulative effect. It validated the work of artisans and distillers who had been laboring quietly for decades. It gave consumers permission to explore traditions they had once dismissed. And it laid the foundation for a pairing culture that would soon transform individual indulgence into shared connoisseurship.

In short, popular culture didn't just reflect the renaissance. It accelerated it.

## IV. Connecting the Bourbon and Cigar Booms

By the late 1990s, cigars and bourbon had not only recovered from decades of decline. They had become intertwined. What began as separate revivals, rooted in tradition and craft, evolved into a shared cultural movement. This convergence wasn't just symbolic or aesthetic; it was sensory, experiential, and deeply intentional.

Cigar lounges began offering bourbon flights; distilleries hosted cigar-pairing events. The ritualistic nature of both experiences—slow, deliberate, rich in flavor and story—made them natural companions. Each heightened the other: bourbon's warmth amplified a cigar's spice; a creamy Connecticut wrapper softened a high-proof rye's intensity. This wasn't casual consumption—it was a performance of taste, heritage, and discernment.

The emerging pairing culture offered enthusiasts a new kind of connoisseurship. Flavor notes were dissected, textures discussed, and ideal combinations debated. The lexicon of wine tasting—"mouthfeel," "finish," "balance," "structure"—was repurposed to describe the chemistry between a bourbon's profile and a cigar's construction. This wasn't just marketing; it was the formalization of a new cultural genre.

*Cigar Aficionado* featured bourbon reviews alongside cigar spreads and helped solidify the two as part of the same aspirational lifestyle. Where once cigars and bourbon occupied separate spaces—one in drawing rooms, the other in hunting cabins—they now appeared together in the same lounges, in the same photo shoots, and in the hands of the same cultural tastemakers.

The convergence wasn't accidental. Both industries saw strategic value in mutual elevation. Cigar makers leaned into bourbon's resurgence to amplify their own credibility; bourbon distillers embraced cigar pairings to anchor their products in luxury and tradition.[16] The result was a powerful feedback loop: a revival that transcended industry lines and created a broader movement rooted in craft, experience, and sensory storytelling.

By decade's end, cigars and bourbon were no longer just back—they were bonded. What emerged was not simply a return to form, but the birth of a new American ritual.

## V. The Boutique Cigar Movement

The boutique cigar movement marked a return to craftsmanship and experimentation, building on traditions reshaped by exile, innovation, and the pursuit of quality. Just as bourbon distillers embraced small-batch and single-barrel releases to reclaim lost prestige, cigar makers turned to artisanal methods to elevate the art of rolling and blending.

Producers like Arturo Fuente, Padron, and La Aurora fused generations of inherited expertise with bold experimentation, setting new standards for non-Cuban cigars. Their meticulous attention to detail—blend selection, aging, wrapper quality—echoed the precision and care seen in bourbon's small-batch revival, where flavor depth outweighed production volume.

This wave of excellence extended beyond legacy names. Independent makers entered the scene with fresh energy, embracing risk and transparency. They experimented with hybrid tobaccos and curing innovations, proudly showcasing their growing regions, processes, and

---

[16] Throughout the 1990s and early 2000s, distilleries such as Maker's Mark, Buffalo Trace, and Woodford Reserve collaborated with cigar lounges and lifestyle publications to promote curated pairings. Maker's Mark co-hosted cigar dinners with *Cigar Aficionado*, while Woodford Reserve and Buffalo Trace appeared in premium pairing menus at lounges like Club Macanudo. Julian Van Winkle III often emphasized the compatibility of his wheated bourbons with fine cigars, reinforcing Pappy Van Winkle's brand identity as both rare and ritualistic.

blends. Like their bourbon counterparts, these boutique cigar makers invited a new kind of consumer: one who sought narrative, nuance, and authenticity.

Transparency became a defining feature, as discerning smokers demanded to know the origins, composition, and craft behind each cigar. Like bourbon enthusiasts tracking mash bills and aging techniques, cigar lovers developed fluency in tobaccos, wrappers, and fermentation styles, ushering in a new vocabulary of connoisseurship.

Nicaragua quickly became a nerve center of boutique excellence. Its regions—Jalapa, Estelí, and Condega—offered ideal soil and climate for growing bold, flavorful tobaccos. Nicaraguan cigars soon rivaled and, in many eyes, surpassed Cuban cigars in strength, complexity, and range. The Dominican Republic, home to brands like Davidoff, also proved that world-class cigars could thrive outside Cuban borders, while the U.S. revival of Connecticut Shade and Broadleaf provided elegant wrappers and earthy Maduros prized in high-end blends.

Limited editions became another signature of the boutique ethos. Small-batch cigars made from rare or aged tobaccos were marketed much like collectible bourbons—coveted, numbered, and often sold out on release. The same consumers chasing elusive bottles of Pappy Van Winkle were also lining up for the latest Fuente Opus X or Padron Anniversary Series.

The 1990s also witnessed the rise of cigar festivals, specialty shops, and enthusiast events. *Cigar Aficionado's* "Big Smoke," among others, gave boutique producers platforms to engage directly with a growing base of educated, passionate consumers. These gatherings mirrored bourbon's own emerging culture of tastings, tours, and collector meetups, each reinforcing the idea that these were not just products but experiences rooted in legacy and mastery.

## The Iconic Fuente Fuente OpusX

*Fuente Fuente OpusX, renowned for their rich flavor and impeccable construction, have become a symbol of luxury and craftsmanship in the cigar world.*

Introduced in 1995, the Fuente Fuente OpusX was the first Dominican puro to gain international acclaim, challenging the dominance of Cuban cigars. Crafted entirely from Dominican-grown tobacco at Chateau de la Fuente, it showcased the potential of Dominican wrappers, previously deemed unsuitable for premium cigars.

The OpusX's bold, full-bodied profile and complex flavors quickly garnered a dedicated following. Its limited production and high demand have made it a coveted item among aficionados, often fetching premium prices on the secondary market.

As cigar lounges gained popularity, the pairing of boutique cigars with premium bourbons became a cultural fixture. The alliance was more than incidental. It was organic. Smokers drawn to the complexity of a well-aged cigar were naturally inclined toward the layered warmth of a high-proof bourbon. Together, they created a ritual of slowness, refinement, and reverence for craft.

More than a comeback, the boutique cigar movement redefined the industry's future. By choosing craft over volume and innovation over nostalgia, producers proved that authenticity still commands loyalty, and set the stage for cigars and bourbon to rise together as icons of American craftsmanship.

# VI. The Premiumization of Bourbon

Bourbon's revival in the 1990s sparked a wave of innovation that redefined the spirit's identity. As small-batch credibility took hold, a movement toward "premiumization" emerged. Distillers expanded the boundaries of aging, flavor, and technique, recasting bourbon as a luxury good rooted in craft but open to creative evolution.

Several factors fueled this evolution. Chief among them was the rise of an educated, enthusiastic consumer base—drinkers who prized complexity, provenance, and artisanal technique. These connoisseurs didn't just tolerate higher prices for quality bourbon; they actively sought out rare, limited-edition releases that delivered something unique. In doing so, they elevated bourbon from a fading legacy spirit into a luxury good worthy of collection, celebration, and ritual.

Inspired by Scotch whisky traditions, American distillers began aging bourbon in barrels previously used for port, sherry, and wine, creating new layers of dried fruit, spice, and toasted sweetness that enriched bourbon's classic vanilla-caramel base. These finishes didn't just expand flavor. They enhanced pairing potential. Port casks, in particular, yielded bourbons whose velvety sweetness matched perfectly with Maduro cigars, while sherry finishes complemented medium-bodied blends with fruit-forward warmth. Toasted barrels, which offered subtler spice and depth, appealed to connoisseurs seeking nuanced harmony between spirit and smoke.

These innovations represented a genuine creative leap, an attempt to explore bourbon's full flavor potential while maintaining its historical identity. By highlighting craftsmanship and sensory sophistication, distillers succeeded in positioning bourbon as a rival to the world's finest spirits.

This evolution gave rise to a new kind of collector culture. Enthusiasts flocked to online forums, tasting events, and whiskey clubs in search of limited releases—none more coveted than Pappy Van Winkle's Family Reserve, which transformed from a niche offering into a cultural icon. Collecting bourbon became more than a pastime; it signified connoisseurship, cultural capital, and refined taste.

Distilleries recognized the opportunity to deepen consumer connection through immersive experiences, inviting fans to walk historic grounds, sample exclusive releases, and engage directly with the artistry of distillation through guided storytelling.

Bourbon bars sprang up across the country, catering to this growing demand. With extensive menus and knowledgeable staff, these venues offered curated tastings that elevated the bourbon experience to new heights. Many of these establishments also featured cigar pairings, cementing the bond between the two industries. Lounges where patrons could sip rare bourbons while enjoying boutique cigars became havens of connoisseurship, spaces where sensory appreciation met cultural tradition.

Of course, premiumization brought growing pains. Soaring demand quickly outpaced supply, creating scarcity that drove up prices and limited access. While some distillers expanded production, others chose to maintain tight allocations to preserve exclusivity. In either case, the scarcity only heightened allure.

Still, the broader effect was transformative. The premiumization movement restored bourbon's prestige, deepened its connection to craftsmanship and culture, and fostered a consumer environment that embraced innovation without sacrificing authenticity.

For cigar makers, bourbon's renaissance was a welcome parallel. The emphasis on heritage, rarity, and ritual made premium bourbon the perfect companion to boutique cigars. Whether enjoyed in lounges, festivals, or private cellars, the pairing of the two became a ritual of depth and discernment.

By the close of the decade, bourbon stood shoulder to shoulder with cigars—not merely revived, but reimagined. Together, they embodied a new standard of American craft, where heritage met innovation and ritual met refinement.

**Antebellum** - *An Antebellum No. 1 cigar and a pour of bourbon rest on charred oak—echoes of fire, craft, and time. A quiet ritual where past and present meet in smoke and grain.*

## Native Pairing — All-American Cigars and Bourbon's Flavor Logic

As bourbon reclaimed its identity through heritage mash bills and small-batch expressions, a quieter movement in the cigar world mirrored that revival: the return to American-grown tobaccos. This wasn't mere nostalgia, but a recovery of a shared sensory grammar—flavor, aroma, and texture—that once naturally aligned cigar tobacco with American whiskey.

Among the most historically resonant examples are *Antebellum cigars*, modern blends inspired by the 19th-century cigars smoked in frontier taverns and gentlemen's clubs. Built around Connecticut, Pennsylvania, and other domestic leaves, these cigars offer earthy, spiced, and toasted profiles that echo the signatures of barrel-aged bourbon. In the mid-1800s, such pairings weren't curated—they were common. Cigar and whiskey producers often came from the same regions and served overlapping tastes.

The significance goes beyond history. These all-American blends—whether rustic or refined—demonstrate how domestic tobaccos can match bourbon's layered, regional complexity while standing apart from imported cigars. They also preview a broader claim made in Part II: that bourbon and cigar pairing is not just a luxury ritual, but a palate-driven system rooted in chemistry, craft, and culture.

## Conclusion: An Interwoven Renaissance

The 1990s revival of bourbon and cigars was more than a nostalgic return. It was a reinvention. Both industries, long dismissed or commodified, reasserted their value through a renewed emphasis on authenticity, craftsmanship, and creative innovation. What began as independent renaissances soon converged, producing a cultural and sensory synergy that elevated both to new heights.

This interconnection wasn't accidental. Bourbon distillers pushed boundaries with small-batch releases, experimental barrel finishes, and heritage-driven storytelling. Cigar makers responded with bold blends, refined fermentation, and an artisanal ethos that mirrored bourbon's revival. Together, they redefined what it meant to pursue excellence—not through mass appeal, but through detail, depth, and narrative.

By the decade's end, a new pairing culture had emerged. Bourbon bars and cigar lounges offered curated experiences where flavor, texture, and aroma were celebrated, not just consumed. Aged Maduro cigars and port-finished bourbons, creamy Connecticut wrappers and wheated whiskeys—these weren't just combinations; they were compositions. The act of pairing became ritualized, blending history, pleasure, and discernment into a distinctly American expression of luxury.

Perhaps most powerfully, both industries learned to tell stories, not just of origin but of transformation. Brands like Pappy Van Winkle, Buffalo Trace, Padron, and Fuente invited consumers into legacies reborn through innovation. The result was a renaissance not just of products, but of meaning.

What began as cultural rediscovery now invites scientific inquiry. The next chapter explores the sensory logic—molecular, psychological, and experiential—that makes bourbon and cigars not just compatible but extraordinary when enjoyed together.

# PART II

# CHAPTER 6

# The Sensory Connection
*Why Bourbon & Cigars Work Together*

The pairing of bourbon and cigars is more than cultural tradition. It is a carefully crafted sensory experience built on the interplay of chemistry and artisanal expertise. Central to their compatibility are shared compounds such as tannins, sugars, oils, and phenolic elements, which together create a complex harmony of taste, aroma, and texture.

This chapter explores the science underlying this remarkable pairing. By examining flavor profiles, retrohaling techniques, mouthfeel, and sensory interactions, we uncover the reasons behind their mutual enhancement. We will also delve into the fascinating parallels between bourbon aging and tobacco fermentation, processes that similarly transform raw materials into refined indulgences.

The art of pairing involves appreciating both the contrasts and synergies between bourbon and cigars. From the robust, earthy notes of a Maduro cigar to the smooth, caramel sweetness of aged bourbon, their beauty emerges through complexity. By understanding the chemical and sensory foundations that unite these two indulgences, we deepen our appreciation for why bourbon and cigars remain a timelessly captivating duo.

# I. The Chemistry of Smoke & Spirit

The compatibility of bourbon and cigars is not just a matter of personal preference or cultural association. It is grounded in a fascinating interplay of chemical compounds that influence taste, aroma, and mouthfeel. Both bourbon and cigars owe their distinctive profiles to complex chemical processes involving fermentation, aging, and extraction of flavors. Understanding these processes provides insight into why bourbon and cigars enhance each other when enjoyed together.

## Chemical Profiles and Their Interactions

Bourbon and cigars are composed of various compounds that contribute to their flavor, aroma, and texture. When combined, the chemical properties of each influence how we perceive their individual characteristics, creating a harmonious sensory experience.

*Bourbon's Chemical Profile:*

Bourbon's signature flavors are primarily shaped during its aging process in charred oak barrels. The charring process caramelizes the wood's natural sugars and releases compounds that interact with the alcohol over time:

- **Tannins**: Derived from the oak barrels, tannins contribute astringency and structure to the bourbon, giving it body and complexity.
- **Sugars**: As the bourbon ages, it absorbs caramelized sugars from the charred oak, resulting in flavors of caramel, vanilla, and butterscotch.
- **Phenolic Compounds**: Lignin breakdown during charring produces vanillin, which imparts a sweet, creamy aroma. Other phenolics contribute to spice and smokiness.
- **Lactones**: Produced during aging, lactones add flavors of coconut and woody notes that enhance the bourbon's depth.
- **Esters**: Formed during fermentation, esters provide fruity, floral, and sometimes sweet notes that add layers of complexity.

*Cigar's Chemical Profile*

The flavor profile of a cigar is influenced by the types of tobacco used, how the leaves are cured, fermented, and aged, and even the region where the tobacco is grown.

- **Oils**: Natural oils present in tobacco leaves contribute to a cigar's richness, providing creamy, earthy, or spicy characteristics.
- **Sugars**: Sugars present in the leaves caramelize during curing and fermentation, creating sweet and sometimes fruity undertones.
- **Tannins**: Tobacco leaves also contain tannins, which provide bitterness and balance to sweeter elements, enhancing the overall flavor complexity.
- **Phenolic Compounds**: Similar to bourbon, tobacco's phenolics contribute to its aroma, producing notes of cocoa, coffee, pepper, and earthiness.
- **Terpenes**: Found in tobacco leaves, terpenes provide aromatic compounds that contribute to floral, citrus, or herbal qualities.

*How Tannins, Sugars, and Oils Interact*

The interaction of tannins, sugars, and oils is central to the pairing experience between bourbon and cigars. When consumed together, their chemical compounds influence how flavors are perceived and appreciated.

- **Sweetness and Bitterness Balance**: The natural sweetness of bourbon, derived from sugars extracted from charred oak barrels, balances the bitterness provided by tannins in cigars. This creates a complementary interaction that makes each flavor component more pronounced.
- **Mouthfeel Enhancement**: Oils from the cigar's tobacco coat the palate, enhancing the mouthfeel of bourbon. This oil layer can soften the astringency of high-proof bourbons, making them appear smoother and more rounded.
- **Retrohaling and Aroma Amplification**: Exhaling cigar smoke through the nose (retrohaling) enhances the olfactory experience, amplifying the aromatic compounds in both the cigar and the bourbon. Phenolic compounds and terpenes from the cigar interact with bourbon's esters and phenolics, producing a fuller sensory experience.

## Aging and Fermentation: Parallels and Synergies

The processes of aging bourbon and fermenting tobacco share many similarities. Both involve the transformation of raw materials over time to enhance complexity, smoothness, and depth.

*Bourbon Aging*

Bourbon must be aged in new, charred oak barrels by law. During aging, the spirit expands and contracts with temperature changes, drawing in and releasing compounds from the wood. The result is a deep, layered profile featuring caramel, vanilla, spice, toasted oak, and occasionally floral or fruity notes.

High-proof bourbons retain more concentrated wood-derived flavors, making them ideal for pairing with fuller-bodied cigars.

*Tobacco Fermentation*

After curing, tobacco leaves are piled into large stacks called *pilones*, where heat and humidity cause chemical changes that remove impurities and enhance flavor. Fermentation allows the leaves to develop rich, mature flavors, ranging from earthy and peppery to creamy and sweet, depending on the variety and curing method.

Maduro wrappers, with their characteristically dark and oily appearance, undergo additional fermentation that enhances sweetness and depth.

These aging and fermentation processes create complementary flavor profiles that enhance the overall pairing experience. The vanilla, caramel, and oak notes of bourbon harmonize with the rich, earthy, and spicy tones of premium cigars.

## Comparative Analysis of Flavor Profiles

The key to a successful pairing lies in matching flavor intensities. Bold bourbons pair best with full-bodied cigars, while lighter bourbons complement milder cigars. This balance allows for the appreciation of both products without one overwhelming the other.

For instance, here are common bourbon styles and the cigar categories that complement them:

- **High-Rye Bourbons** (e.g., Four Roses Single Barrel): With their bold spice and peppery kick, they enhance earthy, pepper-forward cigars like Nicaraguan blends or American-grown styles with rustic character.
- **Wheated Bourbons** (e.g., Maker's Mark, Pappy Van Winkle): Their smooth sweetness complements creamy, nutty, or chocolatey cigars, such as Connecticut Shade-wrapped blends or Dominican hybrids.
- **Barrel-Proof or Full-Bodied Bourbons** (e.g., Elijah Craig Barrel Proof, Stagg Jr.): Pair beautifully with strong, full-bodied cigars like Padron or Opus X, where intensity meets structure.
- **All-American Cigar Blends** (e.g., Antebellum cigars): With earthy, spiced, and toasted profiles, these cigars echo 19th-century American palates and align naturally with mid-proof, oak-forward bourbons (typically fall in the 90–100 proof range), offering a layered yet historically grounded pairing experience.

This chemical interplay forms the basis of why bourbon and cigars are so often enjoyed together. Their combined complexity creates an experience greater than the sum of its parts, allowing enthusiasts to explore a diverse array of flavors and aromas.

## II. Aging in Oak Barrels & Tobacco Fermentation: Parallel Processes

The deep, complex flavors found in both bourbon and cigars are not simply a result of raw ingredients. Instead, they are created through transformative processes that involve time, temperature, and skilled craftsmanship. Both bourbon aging and tobacco fermentation rely on natural chemical reactions to enhance flavor, smoothness, and aroma, making them uniquely suited for pairing. Understanding how these processes work—and how they mirror each other—sheds light on why bourbon and cigars create such a powerful sensory combination.

## The Role of Oak Barrels in Bourbon Production

The maturation of bourbon is one of the most critical factors in developing its rich, multifaceted flavor profile. By law, bourbon must be aged in new, charred oak barrels, a requirement that profoundly influences the spirit's character.

### *The Science of Bourbon Aging*

The interaction between bourbon and the charred oak barrel involves a series of chemical reactions that gradually transform the spirit's flavor, aroma, and color.

- **Tannin Extraction**: Oak wood contains tannins, which are bitter, astringent compounds that contribute structure and dryness to the bourbon. During aging, tannins are slowly released from the wood and interact with the bourbon's alcohol, creating a balanced mouthfeel. Tannins also react with certain compounds in the bourbon to form esters, enhancing aromatic complexity.
- **Sugars and Vanillin**: The charring process caramelizes the wood's natural sugars, creating compounds such as vanillin, which imparts sweet, creamy notes reminiscent of vanilla, caramel, and butterscotch. Over time, the bourbon absorbs these compounds, which are essential to creating the characteristic sweetness of well-aged bourbons.
- **Phenolic Compounds**: Phenolics are released from the oak during the aging process, contributing spicy, smoky, and woody notes. The breakdown of lignin, a structural component of wood, creates phenols that contribute earthy, toasted, and smoky flavors.
- **Lactones and Esters**: Lactones, also known as oak lactones, are responsible for bourbon's coconut and woody characteristics. Esters, formed through the interaction of alcohol and organic acids, provide fruity and floral notes, adding complexity to the overall flavor profile.

- **Temperature and Time**: Seasonal temperature changes cause the bourbon to expand and contract within the barrel, drawing in and pushing out liquid through the wood's charred surface. This constant interaction with the wood accelerates the extraction of flavors and the breakdown of compounds, intensifying the bourbon's character over time.

The result of this aging process is a spirit with an intricate balance of sweetness, spice, woodiness, and creaminess. The richness of aged bourbon provides a perfect counterpoint to the smokiness and earthiness of a well-made cigar.

## Tobacco Fermentation

The journey from raw tobacco leaf to a refined cigar is equally complex. After the tobacco leaves are harvested, they undergo a curing process to remove moisture, but the true transformation occurs during fermentation. This carefully controlled process is essential to developing the rich, smooth, and nuanced flavors that distinguish high-quality cigars.

### The Science of Tobacco Fermentation

Fermentation is not merely a drying process; it is a biochemical transformation that breaks down impurities and enhances the tobacco's natural characteristics.

- **Enzymatic and Microbial Processes**: Tobacco leaves are stacked in large piles known as pilones, where natural heat generated by microbial activity initiates the fermentation process. The process breaks down harsh organic compounds like ammonia and other impurities that would otherwise result in a bitter or acrid taste.
- **Temperature Control**: The temperature within the pilones is carefully monitored and regulated. When the internal heat reaches specific thresholds, the stacks are rotated and rearranged to ensure even fermentation. This meticulous attention to temperature prevents the leaves from overheating, which could destroy delicate flavors.

- **Flavor Development**: As fermentation progresses, the tobacco's chemical structure changes, resulting in enhanced sweetness, richness, and complexity. The breakdown of starches into sugars creates subtle sweetness, while the release of oils contributes to creaminess and texture.
- **Aging and Maturation**: After fermentation, many premium tobaccos are aged for extended periods to allow their flavors to mellow and integrate fully. Like bourbon, the aging process helps eliminate harshness and promotes the development of desirable flavor characteristics.
- **Different Tobacco Varieties**: Maduro wrappers, for instance, undergo prolonged fermentation to achieve their dark, oily appearance and rich, earthy flavor. Connecticut Shade leaves, by contrast, are processed to preserve their smooth, mild qualities.

## Comparing Bourbon Aging and Tobacco Fermentation

The parallels between bourbon aging and tobacco fermentation are striking. Both transform raw, often harsh, materials into refined products through time, careful monitoring, and skilled craftsmanship. Just as a master distiller determines the optimal aging period for bourbon, a master blender decides when tobacco leaves have reached their peak maturity. Both crafts demand patience, experience, and a deep understanding of how chemical processes influence flavor.

Additionally, both processes enhance the interaction between tannins, sugars, oils, and phenolic compounds, creating rich and complementary flavor profiles. The toasted, smoky, and caramelized notes of aged bourbon often complement the earthy, peppery, and creamy flavors found in fermented tobacco.

# III. The Role of Retrohaling & Mouthfeel in Pairing

The sensory connection between bourbon and cigars is more than just a matter of taste; it involves the intricate interaction of aroma, texture, and the entire olfactory system. While the previous sections have focused on the chemical processes that contribute to flavor, this section delves into the art of experiencing those flavors through techniques that enhance enjoyment and deepen the appreciation of the pairing. Two of the most significant aspects of this sensory interplay are retrohaling and mouthfeel, each playing a crucial role in how bourbon and cigars complement each other so effectively.

## Retrohaling in Cigar Smoking

Retrohaling—exhaling cigar smoke through the nose—intensifies the aromatic experience by directly engaging olfactory receptors, allowing the full aromatic profile of the cigar to be appreciated more vividly than through inhalation alone.

Because olfactory receptors distinguish thousands of aromatic compounds compared to the limited categories detected by taste alone, retrohaling provides a richer, more nuanced experience of a cigar's flavor.

When retrohaling, the smoker can detect notes that might otherwise be missed if only tasted through the palate. For example:

- **Pepper and Spice**: These notes are commonly found in cigars with Nicaraguan and Dominican tobacco, where volcanic soil enhances the sharpness and complexity of the leaf. Similar profiles can be found in Pennsylvania Broadleaf and other select tobaccos, which offer peppery undertones and rustic strength when blended skillfully.
- **Cocoa and Coffee**: Commonly detected in Maduro-wrapped cigars, where the extended fermentation process deepens the natural sweetness and richness of the tobacco. Connecticut Broadleaf, a staple of American-grown Maduro cigars, is especially prized for its chocolatey, coffee-like depth on the retrohale.
- **Floral and Earthy Tones**: Particularly present in Connecticut Shade cigars, where the lighter wrapper delivers subtle, aromatic notes that are enhanced through retrohaling. These domestically grown wrappers

offer a creamy, mild retrohale that pairs especially well with wheated bourbons and lighter expressions.

- **All-American blends** that use a mix of Connecticut, Pennsylvania, and other tobaccos often reveal retrohale notes of toasted grain, nutmeg, or dry oak, flavor elements that closely align with the barrel-aged complexity of mid-proof bourbons.

By engaging the olfactory system, retrohaling reveals the cigar's full aromatic complexity and enhances the understanding of how cigar flavors interact harmoniously with bourbon.

Retrohaling is more than just a technique; it is a skill that requires practice and patience. It also serves as a bridge between the cigar and the bourbon, enhancing how the two are experienced together.

## Mouthfeel in Bourbon Tasting

While retrohaling enhances the experience of cigars, mouthfeel plays an equally important role in bourbon tasting. Mouthfeel, referring to bourbon's texture and viscosity on the palate, ranges from light and smooth to heavy and creamy, significantly influencing pairing choices.

The mouthfeel of bourbon is heavily influenced by several factors:
- **Proof**: Higher-proof bourbons (above 100 proof) tend to have a fuller, richer mouthfeel with a more pronounced warming sensation. This robust character often pairs well with full-bodied cigars, where bold flavors complement the intensity of the bourbon.
- **Aging Process**: The longer a bourbon is aged, the more interaction it has with the charred oak barrel, resulting in a silkier, more velvety mouthfeel. Extended aging also produces complex layers of flavor that complement aged cigars.
- **Mash Bill**: The grain composition of bourbon—whether primarily corn, rye, wheat, or barley—impacts its texture. Rye-heavy bourbons often have a spicier, sharper mouthfeel, while wheated bourbons are

known for their smoothness and creamy texture.

Cigar smoke coats the palate with oils and tannins which then interact with bourbon's texture, heightening the richness and complexity of both.

For example, a bourbon with a higher rye content may intensify the peppery notes of a Nicaraguan cigar, while a wheated bourbon may complement the creamy, nutty flavors of a Connecticut Shade cigar. The interplay between the bourbon's texture and the cigar's smoke is what makes pairing such an engaging and rewarding experience.

## Creating a Layered Sensory Experience

When enjoyed together, retrohaling and mouthfeel work synergistically to enhance the sensory experience of bourbon and cigars. The experience begins by tasting bourbon and noting its mouthfeel and flavors, followed by a cigar draw that layers oils and tannins on the palate. Retrohaling then reveals aromatic complexities, deepening flavor perception. Each subsequent sip of bourbon becomes enhanced by residual cigar notes, creating a continuous, multidimensional sensory loop.

Additionally, the pairing process is not merely about combining two products but about amplifying their best qualities. The peppery bite of a high-proof bourbon may enhance the rich, dark chocolate notes of a Maduro cigar, while the creamy smoothness of a wheated bourbon may complement the delicate floral notes of a Connecticut Shade cigar.

By understanding how retrohaling and mouthfeel interact, enthusiasts can create combinations that elevate the experience beyond mere consumption, turning it into an exploration of craftsmanship, tradition, and sensory enjoyment.

## Synthesis: The Sensory Logic Behind the Pairing

Taken together, the shared chemistry, complementary textures, and deliberate pacing of bourbon and cigars create a uniquely immersive experience. Their interaction is no accident. It reflects compatible compounds, mirrored aging, and a natural balance of taste, aroma, and feel. But to fully understand why this pairing endures, we must turn to the act of savoring itself.

# IV. The Art of Savoring

Pairing bourbon and cigars is a ritualized sensory experience that evokes tradition and celebrates craftsmanship. The art of savoring these two indulgences requires mindfulness, patience, and a deliberate approach that goes beyond mere consumption. To truly appreciate a fine bourbon and a premium cigar is to engage in a ritual of appreciation, one that bridges history, culture, and sensory enjoyment.

## The Ritual of Pairing

Enjoying bourbon and cigars begins with selecting products based on their characteristics and compatibility.

Lighting the cigar involves carefully toasting and gently drawing, releasing aromas that mingle harmoniously with the bourbon. Meanwhile, pouring a glass of bourbon is often accompanied by swirling the amber liquid, examining its viscosity, and inhaling the rich bouquet of aromas that rise from the glass.

The ritual continues as the cigar and bourbon are enjoyed together, each puff and sip revealing new layers of flavor. The process is slowed down deliberately, allowing the palate time to adjust and appreciate how the two components interact. Retrohaling adds another dimension to this experience, enhancing the perception of flavor and deepening the sensory connection.

## Pacing and Mindfulness

Bourbon and cigars are inherently tied to slow pacing, allowing their sensory qualities to unfold gradually. This deliberate approach requires mindfulness, a conscious effort to focus on the moment and appreciate the intricate interplay of flavors.

Pacing also helps the palate adjust to the intensity of both bourbon and cigar smoke. By taking small sips of bourbon and alternating with gentle draws from the cigar, enthusiasts can build a gradual, evolving experience that highlights the best qualities of each.

A calm, quiet environment supports mindfulness, enhancing the sensory experience. Whether enjoyed alone or in good company, the process encourages reflection and appreciation, providing an escape from the fast pace of modern life.

## Enhancing the Pairing Through Deliberate Appreciation

Appreciating bourbon and cigars involves understanding their craftsmanship and historical origins, enriching the sensory experience. The more knowledgeable the enthusiast, the more complete the experience becomes.

This process of deliberate appreciation involves:
- **Observation**: Visually examining bourbon color, clarity, cigar construction, and smoke texture.
- **Nosing**: Identifying aromatic components from both bourbon and cigar smoke.
- **Tasting**: Allowing bourbon and cigar smoke to interact slowly on the palate.
- **Reflection**: Considering how each product enhances the other and connects to cultural traditions.

Part of this appreciation also lies in understanding how the interaction between bourbon and cigars is influenced by factors like proof, body, strength, and complexity. High-proof bourbons may intensify the boldness of a Maduro cigar, while milder bourbons may complement the subtlety of a Connecticut Shade. The exploration of these combinations is itself a ritual, one that rewards patience and curiosity.

## Cultural and Sensory Significance

Savoring bourbon and cigars connects enthusiasts to centuries-old traditions associated with leisure, sophistication, and ritualized enjoyment. From Southern gentlemen sipping bourbon on verandas to cigar lounges where enthusiasts gather to exchange knowledge, these products have served as symbols of craftsmanship and refined pleasure.

This cultural dimension adds to the significance of the pairing. Enjoying a fine bourbon and a premium cigar is about more than just taste; it is about participating in a tradition of appreciation that has been passed down through generations. This continuity of enjoyment is part of what makes the experience so meaningful.

Moreover, the sensory experience of pairing bourbon and cigars can be seen as a form of art. The process of selecting, preparing, and enjoying these products requires skill, attention to detail, and a deep respect for the craft. Whether enjoyed alone or shared with others, the ritual offers a sense of connection—not only to the products themselves but also to the history and culture they represent.

## The Art of Savoring as a Personal Journey

The art of savoring is about discovering personal preferences and developing an individual style; there are no hard rules, only guidelines. The beauty of pairing bourbon and cigars lies in the journey of exploration and refinement.

As enthusiasts become more attuned to the subtleties of flavor, aroma, and texture, they deepen their appreciation for the craftsmanship behind each product. This journey of discovery is a central part of the art of savoring, one that continues to evolve with every new pairing.

## Conclusion: Where Tradition Meets Chemistry

This chapter has shown that the pairing of bourbon and cigars is more than cultural. It is a convergence of chemistry, craftsmanship, and sensory design. Shared compounds like tannins, phenolics, esters, and essential oils interact on the palate and through retrohaling to create a complex, layered experience. Parallel processes of aging and fermentation further deepen this compatibility, enriching aroma, flavor, and texture on both sides of the pairing.

Just as important is the ritual of savoring, an act defined by mindfulness, pacing, and deliberate appreciation. From the warmth of bourbon to the aromatic oils of a cigar, each element amplifies the other, forming a feedback loop of sensory enjoyment.

To understand this compatibility at a deeper level, we now turn to the molecular logic behind it. Chapter 7 will break down the chemical compounds and interactions that explain why certain bourbons complement specific cigars, offering new insights into how science informs the art of pairing.

# CHAPTER 7

# Molecular Flavor Interactions

*The Science of Taste and Aroma*

The pairing of **bourbon and cigars** becomes even more compelling when viewed through the lens of molecular science. This chapter explores how compounds like phenols, esters, and terpenes interact across the senses—creating layered experiences of flavor, aroma, and texture.

---

### Don't Worry — You Don't Need a Chemistry Degree

Let's be honest. Some readers might feel tempted to skip a chapter that dives into the molecular chemistry of flavor and aroma. But don't worry: you don't need to memorize compounds or scientific jargon to appreciate what's going on.

The key idea is simple: there *are* scientific factors that shape how bourbon and cigars interact. You don't have to focus on the details, just know that behind the richness of taste and aroma lies a fascinating interplay of molecules. Like most great experiences, pairing is part objective, part subjective—part science, part art, and always a little bit perception.

---

Great pairings begin with molecular interactions: aromatic compounds stimulating both palate and nose. The brain integrates these signals through cross-modal perception, turning taste, smell, and mouthfeel into a unified experience. The harmony between bourbon and cigars isn't just pleasurable. It's grounded in real, measurable chemistry.

## Your Guide to the Chemistry Behind the Pairing

This roadmap offers a quick overview of the chapter's key concepts, from the compounds that shape flavor to how the brain blends taste and aroma. Use it as a reference as you explore how bourbon and cigars interact through structure, scent, and sensation.

---

### Flavor Pairing Roadmap — Your Guide to the Chemistry Behind the Pairing

**I. The Flavor Builders**

How key molecules shape the pairing experience:

◆ **Phenols** → structure, spice, smoke

◆ **Terpenes** → aroma, nuance, complexity

◆ **Esters** → sweetness, softness, fruit

**II. How They Interact**

The chemistry of flavor synergy and contrast

✔ **Shared compounds** = harmony and resonance

✔ **Contrasting profiles** = bold, layered complexity

✔ **Ethanol** = flavor extractor and amplifier

**III. How the Brain Makes Sense of It**

Why it all tastes better together

👃 **Retrohaling** = intensifies aroma perception

🧩 **Cross-modal perception** = taste + smell + mouthfeel → unified experience

### IV. Practical Pairing in Action

Real-world strategies for crafting a perfect match

🎯 **Match profiles**: wheated bourbon + creamy cigar

⚖️ **Use contrast**: spicy rye + earthy Maduro

🔥 **Choose proof and mouthfeel intentionally**

### Conclusion: Where Science Meets Ritual

The perfect pairing is more than preference—it's chemistry, tradition, and sensory design in sync.

---

# I. The Language of Flavor: Phenolic Compounds, Terpenes, and Esters

The rich pairing of bourbon and cigars is grounded in a trio of molecular compounds—phenols, terpenes, and esters—each shaping how we experience flavor and aroma. These molecules form the backbone of taste and scent, preparing the palate for the layered complexity of an intentional pairing.

## Phenolic Compounds: Depth and Structure

Phenolic compounds give bourbon and cigars their smoky, spicy, and earthy backbone. In bourbon, they originate in charred oak barrels and include vanillin (sweet), tannins (dry), and guaiacol (woody). In cigars, they develop during fermentation, producing bold flavors like espresso, pepper, and leather, especially in long-fermented wrappers like Maduro and Broadleaf.

When paired, phenolics from bourbon and cigar can mirror or contrast, either softening intensity or sharpening earthiness, depending on their profiles.

**Terpenes: The Aromatic Bridge**

Terpenes are aromatic molecules that create floral, citrus, herbal, and spice notes. Bourbon gains terpenes from grains and oak (e.g., limonene, linalool, pinene), while cigar terpenes stem from natural leaf oils (e.g., myrcene, caryophyllene, humulene). These shared or complementary terpenes help build a bridge between the two, linking citrus to sweetness, or pepper to spice.

**Esters: Sweetness and Softness**

Esters form during fermentation and aging, delivering fruity and buttery notes: apple (ethyl acetate), banana (isoamyl acetate), and creaminess (butyl acetate). Bourbon typically contains more esters than cigars, but aged tobacco does yield hints of cocoa, molasses, and dried fruit. In combination, esters can soften a spicy cigar or elevate subtle sweetness, especially in wheated or barrel-finished bourbons.

Together, phenols provide structure, terpenes offer aroma, and esters add balance. Their combined effects set the stage for the nuanced interactions explored in the next section.

# II. Terpene & Ester Interactions: Creating Harmony and Contrast

While phenolic compounds provide the backbone of flavor, it's the aromatic dance of terpenes and esters that often makes a bourbon-cigar pairing feel truly alive. These molecules spark moments of brightness, softness, contrast, and complexity, elevating both the cigar and the spirit through their interplay.

**Shared Aromatics: The Common Ground**

Bourbon and cigars both contain naturally occurring terpenes, though they come from different places. Bourbon picks them up from grains and charred oak barrels; cigars develop them in the oils of fermented tobacco leaves, shaped by soil, climate, and curing.

Some shared terpenes that shape successful pairings include:

- **Linalool**: light, floral, and lavender-like; found in toasted-barrel bourbons and creamy, mild cigars.
- **Caryophyllene**: spicy and peppery; common in bold cigars and rye-forward bourbons.
- **Humulene**: earthy and woody; ties together aged bourbon and dark-wrapped cigars.
- **Limonene**: bright and citrusy; highlights floral or naturally sweet cigars.

These shared notes act like a familiar melody running through both cigar and bourbon, setting the stage for balance and resonance.

## Complementary Interactions

Pairings often succeed by reinforcing similar notes. For example:

- **Fruity bourbons** (rich in esters like ethyl acetate) pair beautifully with creamy cigars like those with Connecticut Shade wrappers; the cigar's softness lets the bourbon's fruit notes shine.
- **Wheated bourbons**, known for their mellow sweetness, match well with mild, nutty cigars, creating a smooth, unified profile.
- **Herbal or citrus-driven bourbons** bring freshness to naturally sweet cigars, elevating delicate florals or honeyed tobacco.

These combinations work because their aromas and flavors speak the same sensory language.

## Contrasting Interactions

On the other hand, contrast can create a kind of flavorful tension—an interplay that keeps the palate alert:

- A **spicy rye bourbon** can slice through the richness of a Maduro cigar, adding fire to earth.

- **Port- or sherry-finished bourbons** (with nutty, fruity tones) offset the savory depth of aged tobacco, creating a push-pull of sweet and bold.
- A **high-proof bourbon** intensifies the oils and spice of a full-bodied cigar, turning each sip and draw into a layered experience.

The beauty of contrast is that it doesn't compete—it reveals.

### The Role of Ethanol Content and Flavor Amplification

Ethanol plays a pivotal role in bourbon-cigar pairings by acting as a solvent that enhances the perception of flavor.

- **Ethanol Extraction**: During sipping, ethanol draws out aromatic compounds from cigar smoke, especially when retrohaling, intensifying the flavor experience.
- **Warming Effects**: Higher-proof bourbons produce a warming sensation that stimulates the palate and accentuates cigar oils, enriching notes of spice, caramel, and toast.
- **Balancing Act**: Lower-proof bourbons offer a gentler profile, allowing subtler cigar flavors—like cream, florals, or light earthiness—to come forward without being overshadowed.

By understanding how ethanol influences flavor perception, one can better appreciate why certain bourbon-cigar pairings feel more complete and balanced than others.

The synergy between bourbon and cigars arises not only from shared compounds but from their dynamic interactions when enjoyed together. Whether through harmonious enhancement or dynamic contrast, the interplay of terpenes, esters, and ethanol offers an endlessly fascinating palette of possibilities.

We now move to examining how the brain processes taste and aroma to fully understand why bourbon and cigars produce such a powerful sensory experience.

# III. The Neuroscience of Taste and Retrohaling

Pairing bourbon and cigars engages complex sensory systems in the brain, creating an experience that goes beyond simple flavor. By examining the roles of olfactory receptors, gustatory senses, and retrohaling, we can understand how this interplay produces such a powerful effect.

Flavor perception depends significantly on the interaction between olfactory receptors in the nose and taste receptors on the tongue. While taste buds detect basic sensations like sweetness, saltiness, bitterness, sourness, and umami, the true complexity of flavor arises from the olfactory system. Bourbon and cigars, with their intricate flavor profiles, interact with these systems in unique and complementary ways.

## Olfactory Receptors and Flavor Perception

The olfactory system is one of the most powerful sensory mechanisms humans possess. Humans possess about 400 olfactory receptors, enabling detection of thousands of distinct scents. Together, the aromatic molecules in bourbon and cigars stimulate these receptors, creating a nuanced sensory experience.

Bourbon's esters, terpenes, and phenolics—derived from grain and charred oak—and tobacco's aromatic compounds—formed through fermentation and curing—bind to receptors in the nasal cavity and signal the brain's olfactory cortex.

When these aromatic compounds are inhaled, they bind to receptors in the nasal cavity, sending signals to the olfactory bulb and ultimately to the brain's olfactory cortex, where scent perception occurs. Because olfaction is responsible for the majority of what we perceive as flavor, the interaction between bourbon and cigars through scent is a critical aspect of their pairing compatibility.

## Retrohaling as Sensory Integration

Retrohaling engages the olfactory system more directly than standard exhalation, intensifying the aromatic dimension of cigar smoke. When combined with bourbon—especially higher-proof expressions—retrohaling becomes a powerful amplifier of shared aromatic compounds (phenols, esters, and terpenes) that shape the pairing's complexity. This process bridges taste and aroma, forming a cohesive multisensory experience grounded in neurochemical integration.

## Ethanol's Role in Aroma Detection

Ethanol in bourbon enhances aroma detection during retrohaling. As it evaporates, ethanol acts as a solvent that releases aromatic compounds from both the bourbon and the cigar's smoke, making them more perceptible to the olfactory system. The warming sensation of higher-proof bourbons stimulates the palate, intensifying the perception of spice, leather, and cocoa in full-bodied cigars.

This creates a feedback loop: the presence of bourbon enhances cigar flavors, while cigar smoke draws out additional dimensions of the bourbon's character.

## Cross-Modal Perception: Enhancing the Experience

Cross-modal perception—the brain's ability to integrate inputs from multiple senses—explains why bourbon and cigars create such a unified and satisfying experience. Taste, smell, and touch (mouthfeel) converge to shape a holistic impression of flavor.

As bourbon and cigar compounds interact, ethanol amplifies aromatic oils from the cigar, while the bourbon's warmth enhances sensitivity to flavor. Together, these effects generate a layered sensory dialogue that makes pairings feel instinctively harmonious or compellingly dynamic.

The brain combines these sensory inputs to form a holistic impression of the pairing. For instance, the spicy, peppery phenolics in a rye-heavy bourbon may enhance the boldness of a Maduro cigar, while the sweetness of a wheated bourbon can bring out the creamy, nutty qualities of a mild Connecticut Shade cigar.

Cross-modal perception helps explain why some bourbon-cigar pairings feel naturally balanced: the brain integrates complementary aromas and tastes into a unified, satisfying experience. In contrast, well-matched opposites create a dynamic interplay that sharpens flavor perception and leaves a lasting impression.

Retrohaling and cross-modal perception reveal how bourbon and cigars engage the senses in concert, transforming individual components into a unified sensory experience. By understanding how the brain processes these inputs, enthusiasts can craft pairings that are both intentional and deeply rewarding.

The next section puts this science into practice, applying molecular principles to real-world pairing strategies.

## IV. Pairing in Practice: Using Chemistry to Guide Choices

By applying a molecular understanding of bourbon and cigars, enthusiasts can elevate their pairings beyond tradition or guesswork. Phenolic compounds, terpenes, esters, and ethanol each shape how flavor is perceived. Knowing how they interact can help craft pairings that are both balanced and bold.

Whether the goal is harmony or contrast, successful pairings stem from how these compounds align or oppose each other across aroma, texture, and intensity.

## Applying Molecular Knowledge to Pairing

One of the most significant aspects of pairing is acknowledging how the ethanol content of bourbon interacts with the oils and phenolic compounds in cigars. Higher-proof bourbons, for instance, amplify the intensity of certain cigar flavors, enhancing boldness and complexity. Conversely, lower-proof bourbons allow subtler nuances to emerge, making them ideal for milder cigars.

Additionally, the tannins and esters present in bourbon can interact with the natural sugars and oils in tobacco, creating unique flavor combinations that might not be detectable when each product is enjoyed separately.

## Crafting Intentional Pairings: Bourbon Styles & Cigar Matches

While taste remains personal, chemical principles offer practical strategies for crafting memorable bourbon and cigar combinations.

Smooth and mellow wheated bourbons complement mild cigars with creamy or nutty profiles. The bourbon's caramel and vanilla esters highlight the cigar's creamy, nutty tones, while its lower phenolic content ensures the cigar's subtle flavors remain distinct.

The velvety mouthfeel of wheated bourbon further amplifies the cigar's soft texture, allowing the complementary oils and esters to integrate into a soothing, harmonious experience.

*Rye-Heavy Bourbons with Bold Cigars (e.g., Maduro or Broadleaf)*

Rye-heavy bourbons, known for their spicy phenolic compounds and bold character, pair naturally with rich, full-bodied cigars such as those wrapped in Maduro or Broadleaf. Spirits like Wild Turkey 101 or Knob Creek intensify the earthy, leathery, and cocoa notes of these cigars, while their high-proof warmth and tannic structure deepen the overall experience.

Retrohaling completes the pairing, revealing additional layers of pepper and spice as the cigar's smoke and the bourbon's aromatic compounds converge in the olfactory pathway, enhancing depth and complexity.

*Barrel-Finished Bourbons with Aged Cigars*

As the popularity of bourbon continues to grow, many distilleries have experimented with barrel finishes, such as port, sherry, or toasted barrels. These barrel finishes impart notes of dark fruit, chocolate, and nuttiness, enhancing specific cigar profiles.

For instance, bourbons finished in port barrels (like Angel's Envy) often have a rich, fruity quality that pairs well with cigars featuring aged tobacco. Older cigars, particularly those with Maduro or Broadleaf wrappers, benefit from bourbon's wine-like notes, complementing their deep, leathery, and nutty characteristics.

Sherry-finished bourbons, with their subtle sweetness and raisin-like undertones, can enhance the creamy, floral notes of cigars rolled with Connecticut Broadleaf wrappers. By pairing a sherry-finished bourbon with a well-aged cigar, enthusiasts can experience a nuanced interplay where the bourbon's complex flavors accentuate the cigar's rich, aged characteristics.

## Why Certain Pairings Work Well

The most rewarding bourbon-cigar pairings hinge on how their molecular profiles align or contrast. Shared compounds like terpenes and esters create harmony—think fruity bourbons with creamy cigars—while opposing traits, such as a spicy rye with a rich Maduro, generate bold, dynamic contrast.

Ethanol plays a critical role, too: higher-proof bourbons amplify the depth of robust cigars, while lower-proof options highlight subtler cigars without overwhelming them.

Ultimately, pairing is part science, part art—a sensory exploration where chemistry guides intuition, and tradition meets discovery.

## Conclusion: The Fusion of Science and Ritual

Ultimately, the art of pairing bourbon and cigars highlights the timeless allure of craftsmanship, blending tradition with the precision of modern science. Centuries of dedicated fermentation, aging, and blending practices have created products celebrated not only for their sensory pleasure but also for their capacity to deepen life's finer experiences.

Exploring molecular flavor interactions has illuminated why bourbon and cigars complement each other so remarkably. By understanding how phenolic compounds, terpenes, esters, and ethanol engage the palate and olfactory senses, enthusiasts gain a richer appreciation of the deliberate synergy behind exceptional pairings. This scientific framework enhances both the sensory and cultural appreciation, allowing pairings to transcend mere preference and achieve a sophisticated complexity.

Yet, science alone does not define the pairing experience. The interplay among molecular chemistry, personal tastes, cultural heritage, and the mindful rituals of enjoyment gives bourbon and cigar pairings their unique richness. This balance of structure and creativity, of tradition and innovation, is why these pairings endure.

From molecular chemistry, we now turn outward to the broader environmental forces that shape flavor. The next chapter explores how geography, climate, soil composition, and water sources—the elements of terroir—give bourbon and cigars their distinctive identities, from Kentucky's limestone-filtered waters to the volcanic soils of Nicaragua and the Dominican Republic.

CHAPTER 8

# Regional Terroir
*Geography's Flavor Fingerprint*

W hen it comes to bourbon and cigars, the concept of *terroir*—
the influence of geography, soil, climate, and human
craftsmanship— plays a defining role in shaping flavor.
Though most often associated with wine, aficionados of bourbon and
cigars alike recognize that place-specific factors deeply impact complexity
and character.

For bourbon, Kentucky's limestone-rich water and seasonal climate foster
signature notes of caramel, vanilla, spice, and oak. Premium tobacco from
regions like Nicaragua, the Dominican Republic, and Cuba yields diverse
flavor profiles based on soil, altitude, and curing traditions. These regional
distinctions don't just define individual products; they shape the pairing
experience, where unique characteristics can harmonize or contrast to
reveal new dimensions.

Yet terroir is more than nature. It's also craftsmanship. The way bourbon
is aged, blended, and barreled, and how tobacco is fermented, cured, and

rolled, shapes the final expression. In both crafts, producers work in concert with their environment, elevating raw materials through skill and tradition.

This chapter explores how Kentucky's bourbon heritage and the world's leading cigar regions shape their respective flavor identities. By examining the interplay between geography and craftsmanship, we gain insight into why certain pairings resonate, and how the power of place elevates the experience.

# I. The Kentucky Connection: Limestone, Water, and Bourbon's Birthplace

Kentucky's reputation as the heart of bourbon production is far from arbitrary. It is a reality rooted in the state's unique geographical and environmental advantages, which have defined the region's bourbon-making traditions for over two centuries. While bourbon is produced in various states across the United States, the so-called "Bourbon Belt"—stretching from Kentucky into parts of Tennessee, Indiana, and Ohio—has become synonymous with the highest-quality whiskey.

## Limestone-Filtered Water

A defining advantage for Kentucky bourbon is its abundant limestone-filtered water. The region's porous limestone naturally removes iron—an element that can spoil flavor—while enriching the water with calcium and magnesium. These minerals promote healthy fermentation and contribute to the clean, sweet profile bourbon is known for. Many distilleries continue to source water from local springs, reinforcing their bond to the land and grounding their spirits in a sense of place.

## Climate and Aging

Kentucky's seasonal extremes—hot summers and cold winters—create an ideal aging environment. As barrels expand and contract with temperature shifts, bourbon "breathes" in and out of the wood, extracting rich flavors like vanilla, oak, and spice. High humidity reduces evaporation, preserving more spirit and intensifying its character. These natural conditions give Kentucky bourbon a depth and complexity that's hard to replicate elsewhere.

## Bourbon Belt Craftsmanship

While Kentucky remains the undisputed leader in bourbon production, the broader Bourbon Belt also includes Tennessee, Indiana, and parts of Ohio. Each of these regions contributes subtle variations to the whiskey-making tradition, reflecting differences in craftsmanship, regional practices, and local resources.

Tennessee, for example, distinguishes itself from Kentucky bourbon through the Lincoln County Process, a charcoal mellowing technique used before aging. This additional filtration through sugar maple charcoal gives Tennessee whiskey a smoother, slightly sweeter profile that some argue pairs exceptionally well with lighter, floral cigars.

Indiana has also emerged as a key player, particularly through the production of high-rye bourbons known for their bold, spicy character. Meanwhile, Ohio's smaller craft distilleries are experimenting with innovative aging techniques and grain bills that push the boundaries of what bourbon can be.

What varies is the application of tradition and technique, resulting in diverse flavor profiles that appeal to a wide range of palates.

## Pairing Implications

Kentucky's rich, caramel-driven bourbons often pair beautifully with bold Maduro cigars, whose earthy and smoky profiles complement the spirit's deep sweetness. In contrast, lighter bourbons from Tennessee—floral, citrusy, or honeyed—match well with creamy Connecticut Shade cigars, creating a smooth, elegant experience that highlights subtle complexity in both.

Ultimately, the Kentucky Connection represents more than just a geographical advantage—it reflects a centuries-old commitment to craftsmanship and tradition.

## II. The Tobacco Regions: Creating Cigar Diversity

Unlike bourbon's deep roots in the American South, premium cigar tobacco comes from a broad range of global regions, each with its own unique environmental and cultural imprint. Soil, climate, altitude, and curing methods all shape the character of the final cigar, contributing complexity, strength, sweetness, or smoothness.

These regional characteristics are essential to thoughtful pairing. Understanding where and how tobacco is grown allows us to connect specific cigar profiles to bourbons with complementary or contrasting traits, enhancing the overall flavor experience.

### Cuba: A Pre-1962 Legacy

For much of the early 20th century, Cuban cigars were considered the gold standard of the industry. The island's fertile Vuelta Abajo region was particularly renowned for producing rich, earthy, and leathery tobacco, prized for its complexity and smoothness. The combination of Cuba's mineral-rich soil, subtropical climate, and centuries-old growing techniques created a product that was unrivaled in both flavor and consistency.

Even today, Cuban cigars retain a legendary reputation, enhanced by the mystique of the U.S. embargo that began in 1962. That embargo also spurred innovation, as exiled Cuban cigar makers brought their seeds and skills to new soils in the Dominican Republic, Nicaragua, and Honduras, laying the foundation for today's global cigar industry.

The legacy of Cuban cigars continues to set a benchmark for the global industry. Their rich, leathery, and earthy flavors pair classically with bourbons that feature bold, spicy, and oak-driven profiles.

## Dominican Republic

Following the Cuban embargo, the Dominican Republic's fertile Cibao Valley, with its volcanic soil and ideal climatic conditions, became the epicenter of Dominican tobacco production.

Dominican cigars are known for their smooth, creamy, and refined profiles—often milder than their Nicaraguan or Cuban counterparts. Notes of cedar, cream, coffee, and gentle spice are common. The use of hybrid seeds, many with Cuban lineage, has led to an impressive range of flavor expressions. These characteristics make them ideal companions for wheated bourbons and other sweeter whiskey profiles. The softer, more nuanced flavor of the cigar allows the bourbon's caramel and vanilla notes to shine, enhancing the overall pairing experience.

## Nicaragua

If the Dominican Republic is known for smoothness and refinement, Nicaragua is known for power and boldness. The nation's rapidly growing cigar industry is built on the unique characteristics of its volcanic soil, particularly in the regions of Jalapa, Estelí, and Condega. Each area contributes distinct qualities to Nicaraguan tobacco. Jalapa tobacco offers natural sweetness and complexity, ideal for wrappers. Estelí produces bold, peppery leaves that form the heart of many strong blends. Condega adds balance with earthy, nutty tones. Together, these regions define Nicaragua's reputation for powerful, flavor-rich cigars.

The strong, earthy, and peppery qualities of Nicaraguan cigars make them well-suited for pairing with high-proof, rye-forward bourbons. The intense spiciness of the cigar and the bourbon interact dynamically, creating a powerful experience where the heat of the bourbon enhances the cigar's natural oils and intensifies the flavor.

## Honduras

While not as prominent as Nicaragua or the Dominican Republic, Honduras remains a respected cigar-producing region with its own distinctive flavor profile. Tobacco grown in the Jamastran Valley is particularly noted for its earthy, woody, and slightly spicy qualities.

Honduran cigars often occupy a middle ground between the power of Nicaraguan cigars and the smoothness of Dominican offerings. Their moderate spice and earthy tones pair well with medium-bodied bourbons that offer caramel warmth or subtle floral and fruit notes, allowing both cigar and spirit to enhance rather than overpower each other.

## American Terroir: A Tradition of Domestic Tobacco

While the term *terroir* is most often associated with international tobacco regions like Cuba or Nicaragua, the United States possesses its own deeply rooted and distinctive cigar terroirs. From the fertile valleys of Connecticut to the rolling farmlands of Pennsylvania and Kentucky, regional soil, climate, and cultivation methods have shaped some of the world's most prized cigar tobaccos.

### *Connecticut River Valley: Shade & Broadleaf Excellence*

The Connecticut River Valley is home to two of the most iconic wrapper tobaccos in the world—Connecticut Shade and Connecticut Broadleaf. The area's mineral-rich soil and temperate climate, coupled with innovative growing techniques, have created a terroir unlike any other.

Connecticut Shade is grown under cheesecloth canopies that filter sunlight, resulting in thin, delicate leaves with a light golden hue and a creamy, mild flavor. Known for its smooth, buttery texture, this wrapper pairs beautifully with wheated or lower-proof bourbons, allowing subtle vanilla, floral, and nutty notes to emerge in harmony.

Connecticut Broadleaf, by contrast, is bold and rugged. Grown in direct sunlight and harvested late, this tobacco yields thick, dark leaves perfect for Maduro wrappers. Its rich flavor — marked by espresso, dark chocolate, and earth — matches well with high-proof bourbons, rye-heavy mash bills, or barrel-finished expressions. The pairing amplifies depth and intensity, delivering a robust and indulgent experience.

*Pennsylvania: The Amish Legacy of Broadleaf Tobacco*

In the heart of Lancaster County, Pennsylvania's Amish farmers have cultivated a robust style of Broadleaf tobacco for generations. Similar in strength to Connecticut Broadleaf but with a distinct mineral edge, Pennsylvania tobacco contributes deep, smoky, and earthy notes to cigars. It pairs exceptionally well with spicier bourbons and whiskeys aged in heavy-char barrels, creating a flavor union rooted in grit and heritage.

*Kentucky: Fire-Cured Tradition and Flavor*

Kentucky, better known for its bourbon, also produces unique cigar tobacco—especially fire-cured varieties used in blends that feature smoky, barbecue-like undertones. This tobacco, often grown in western Kentucky, is cured using hardwood smoke over open fires, imbuing it with intense, rustic character. When paired with similarly smoky or oak-forward bourbons, Kentucky tobacco adds a regional resonance—a rare but compelling homage to shared soil and shared smoke.

The global diversity of cigar-growing regions offers a wide spectrum of flavors, from bold and peppery to smooth and creamy. Understanding how geography shapes these profiles empowers enthusiasts to craft pairings that bring out the best in both cigar and bourbon.

# III. Regional Flavor Profiles & Pairing Strategies

The origins of bourbon and cigar tobacco shape not just their identity, but their flavor. Whether it's Nicaragua's volcanic soils or Kentucky's limestone-filtered water, terroir leaves an indelible mark. Recognizing these regional influences helps enthusiasts approach pairings with more purpose and precision.

## Matching Profiles to Enhance Similarities

A reliable pairing strategy is to match cigars and bourbons with shared characteristics. This approach emphasizes harmony—letting similar notes amplify one another.

For instance, Nicaraguan cigars, known for their bold, peppery spice, pair seamlessly with rye-heavy bourbons that echo those same flavors through baking spices and herbal heat. The synergy of spice and strength creates a cohesive, full-bodied experience.

At the other end of the spectrum, Connecticut Shade cigars—with their creamy, delicate smoke—elevate the sweetness of wheated bourbons. Notes of caramel, vanilla, and honey glide effortlessly across the palate when paired with such mild cigars, producing a silky, elegant match.

The success of these pairings lies in their ability to enhance similarities. When flavor profiles overlap, the sensory experience becomes richer and more coherent, allowing the enthusiast to appreciate the subtle nuances of each product.

## Contrasting Profiles for Complexity

Pairing opposites can be just as rewarding. Contrasting profiles bring tension and complexity to the experience, often revealing flavors that might otherwise go unnoticed.

Take bold Maduro cigars, with their rich notes of cocoa, leather, and earth. When paired with bourbons finished in port or sherry barrels—offering dried fruit, nuttiness, and sweetness—the contrast produces a decadent, layered interplay of earth and fruit, smoke and sugar.

Another successful contrast lies in pairing spicy, high-proof bourbons with savory cigars. The cigar's leathery depth softens the bourbon's bite, while the whiskey's sweetness cuts through the smoke's intensity, keeping the palate alert and engaged.

Contrasting pairings are especially rewarding when executed with care. Rather than clashing, the differences between bourbon and cigar profiles can enhance each other, creating a sensory experience that feels both balanced and exciting.

### Terroir & Craftsmanship Interplay

Whether matching or contrasting, effective pairings are rooted in a deeper understanding of how flavor is shaped by both terroir and human touch.

In bourbon, limestone-filtered water, seasonal temperature swings, and charred oak barrels all leave their imprint. In cigars, soil fertility, altitude, and curing conditions do the same. A Nicaraguan tobacco leaf grown in Estelí carries the fire of volcanic earth; a Connecticut Shade wrapper reflects the cool restraint of shaded growth.

But terroir alone doesn't create greatness. Distillers and cigar makers refine what nature offers through artistry—selecting yeast strains, managing fermentation, blending tobaccos. When terroir and craftsmanship align across both cigar and bourbon, pairings become more than flavor. They become expression.

The parallel processes of aging, fermentation, and curing provide a framework for understanding how bourbon and cigars can be paired intentionally. When these processes align—whether through shared terroir elements or complementary craftsmanship—the resulting combination can be nothing short of extraordinary.

## Conclusion: Geography's Lasting Influence

The exploration of terroir in bourbon and cigars reveals a central truth: flavor is not merely created—it is cultivated. From Kentucky's limestone-filtered waters to the volcanic soils of Nicaragua, geography imparts character that no technique can fully imitate. But it is through the hands of distillers and cigar makers—those who blend tradition with innovation—that this character becomes an experience. Terroir, then, is not just about where a product comes from. It is about how that place is honored, interpreted, and transformed through craft.

When we pair bourbon and cigars with an awareness of terroir, we engage in more than a sensory exercise. We participate in a living tradition. Each thoughtful pairing becomes a bridge between regions, a conversation between histories, and a celebration of human ingenuity rooted in the land. Whether harmonizing Kentucky caramel with Dominican cream, or contrasting Nicaraguan spice with port-barrel sweetness, the choices we make are enriched by the stories behind them. In this way, terroir connects palate to place, and every pairing becomes a tribute to identity, origin, and craft.

# CHAPTER 9

# Understanding Bourbon Profiles
# & Pairing Strategies

B ourbon and cigars don't just pair well by tradition. They complement each other through measurable sensory dynamics shaped by ingredients, aging, and craftsmanship. In earlier chapters, we explored the molecular interactions (Chapter 7) and regional terroirs (Chapter 8) that define their character. Now, we shift from theory to practice.

This chapter offers a strategic approach to pairing, focusing on how the specific components of bourbon—mash bill, barrel aging, and proof—interact with different cigar styles. Rather than relying on trial and error, we'll use what we've learned to pair intentionally: matching profiles for harmony, contrasting traits for complexity, or balancing intensity for cohesion.

Whether you're reaching for a spicy Nicaraguan cigar or a creamy Connecticut Shade, understanding bourbon profiles is the first step in crafting memorable pairings that elevate both the cigar and the pour.

# I. Foundations of Bourbon Flavor

A thoughtful pairing begins with knowing how bourbon's flavor is built. Three primary elements—grain recipe (mash bill), barrel aging, and proof—combine to produce a bourbon's personality. Recognizing how these variables shape aroma, taste, and mouthfeel gives you the tools to match bourbon with cigars more deliberately.

## Grain Recipes (Mash Bills)

All bourbon starts with at least 51% corn, which imparts natural sweetness. But it's the secondary grains that shape its style:

- **Rye bourbons** are bold and spicy, offering notes of black pepper, cinnamon, and clove, ideal for full-bodied cigars with earth or leather.
- **Wheated bourbons** are soft and smooth, highlighting vanilla, honey, and caramel, perfect with milder cigars like Dominican blends or Connecticut wrappers.
- **High-malt bourbons** add subtle toast, nuttiness, and roundness, complementing cigars with creamy or roasted nut profiles.

These grain-driven signatures help guide cigar selection by matching strength, texture, and key flavor tones.

## Barrel Aging & Finishing

New, charred oak barrels contribute bourbon's familiar layers: caramel, vanilla, spice, and smoke. Younger bourbons tend to be brighter and lighter; older ones develop deeper complexity and structure, qualities that influence how they interact with cigar oils and tannins.

Secondary barrel finishes—such as port, sherry, or toasted oak—introduce dried fruit, chocolate, and nuttiness, opening up pairings with Maduro or Broadleaf cigars that echo those notes.

## Proof (Alcohol by Volume)

Alcohol strength impacts not just intensity, but how flavors are perceived. Higher-proof bourbons (110+) can intensify rich cigars, while lower-proof expressions (80–90) offer balance and clarity when paired with more delicate smokes.

A few drops of water can soften a high-proof pour, revealing subtler flavor layers and improving compatibility with medium-bodied cigars.

# II. Pairing Strategies: Enhancing the Experience

While bourbon's flavor foundations set the stage, it's the interaction with cigars that brings pairing to life. By applying three key strategies— complementing, contrasting, and balancing—you can move beyond guesswork into purposeful combinations where both bourbon and cigar shine. These methods translate the science and terroir explored in earlier chapters into practical, memorable tasting experiences.

## Complementing Pairings: Matching Similarities

Some of the most rewarding pairings emerge when bourbon and cigars echo one another, reinforcing shared notes of sweetness, spice, or creaminess.

Wheated bourbons, with their soft, caramelized profiles, pair beautifully with mild cigars wrapped in Connecticut Shade. The cigar's floral, nutty tones mirror the bourbon's vanilla and honey, creating a smooth, buttery harmony.

Rye-forward bourbons, bold with cinnamon and clove, find their match in Nicaraguan cigars rich in pepper, leather, and earth. Together, they deliver a powerful interplay of spice and strength.

Barrel-finished bourbons open new pairing avenues: sherry casks lend dark fruit and nuttiness that elevate the sweetness of Maduro cigars, while port finishes highlight cocoa and dried fruit in Broadleaf-wrapped blends.

American heritage blends—made from robust American-grown tobacco—align especially well with high-rye bourbons. Its earthy richness and historical depth match the bourbon's spiced intensity, offering a pairing that is both grounded and evocative of early American craft.

Complementary pairings reward those who seek cohesion: flavors that echo, reinforce, and glide together with purpose.

## Contrasting Pairings: Creating Dynamic Interplay

Not every great pairing is about harmony. Some thrive on tension. Contrasting profiles can heighten complexity, sharpen perception, and reveal flavors that might otherwise go unnoticed.

High-proof bourbons, bold with heat and spice, can be tempered by mild, creamy cigars like Connecticut Shade. The cigar's soft draw softens the bourbon's bite, allowing subtler caramel and oak notes to surface.

Conversely, wheated bourbons—smooth and sweet—offer a calming foil to the fiery spice of Nicaraguan or Honduran cigars. The sweetness cools the pepper, while the cigar adds dimension to the bourbon's softness.

Some contrasts are more dramatic still: fire-cured cigars with smoky, barbecue-like intensity paired with sweet, toasted-barrel bourbons creates a vivid interplay of char, sugar, and smoke. Port- or sherry-finished bourbons bring rich fruit and nuttiness to earthy Maduro cigars, producing a layered push-pull of sweetness and strength.

Historic tobacco profiles also lend themselves to contrast. When paired with deeply charred or rye-heavy bourbons, the cigar's cocoa and mineral depth collides with bourbon's spice and heat—an intense, rewarding match that invites slow appreciation.

Contrasting pairings are for those who enjoy a bit of tension in their tasting, a balance struck not through similarity, but through dynamic opposition.

## Balancing Pairings: Achieving Cohesion

When neither harmony nor contrast takes the lead, balance becomes the goal. A well-balanced pairing ensures that bourbon and cigar enhance each other without competing, offering a cohesive, layered experience.

Medium-proof bourbons (90–110) often strike the ideal midpoint: complex enough to hold their own, yet restrained enough not to overwhelm. Paired with medium-bodied cigars—those with earthy, nutty, or woody notes—they allow both elements to unfold gradually, sharing the spotlight.

For higher-proof bourbons, a few drops of water can open up the palate and temper ethanol intensity, allowing more delicate cigar flavors to emerge. This small adjustment often brings the pairing into smoother equilibrium.

Another effective strategy is progression. Beginning with lighter cigars and softer bourbons, and gradually building to bolder pairings, helps the palate acclimate and appreciate each layer. It's not just balance in the glass. It's balance across the entire experience.

American heritage blends embody this approach. Though rich and full-bodied, they pair gracefully with well-aged bourbons that combine depth with structure. The result isn't just power. It's poise.

Balanced pairings reward patience and attention. When done well, they create a conversation between flavors—neither shouting, neither fading, but meeting in a shared and satisfying middle.

# Bourbon & Cigar Flavor Pairing — A Sensory Guide

The Bourbon & Cigar Flavor Wheel visually maps the dominant flavors in bourbon and cigars, helping you identify how profiles align, contrast, or balance in a pairing.

## Wheel Structure

### Left Side: Bourbon Flavors

- Sweet Notes (Amber Tones): Vanilla, caramel, honey, maple syrup, brown sugar.
- Spice Notes (Red Tones): Cinnamon, black pepper, clove, nutmeg, ginger.
- Fruit Notes (Orange Tones): Apple, dried cherry, citrus zest, pear.
- Wood & Smoke (Brown Tones): Oak, cedar, toasted wood, smoke, char.

### Right Side: Cigar Flavors

- Earthy (Green Tones): Leather, soil, bark, mineral.
- Spice (Bright Red): Cayenne, chili, paprika, black pepper.
- Sweet (Gold Tones): Cocoa, coffee, cream, honey, roasted nuts.
- Herbal & Floral (Soft Green): Tea leaf, grass, fresh herbs, blossoms.

### Center: Interaction Zone

- Green Lines: Complementary (shared flavors).
- Yellow Lines: Balanced (contrast in harmony).
- Red Lines: Contrasting (opposites intensify each other).

## How to Use the Wheel in 3 Steps

### 1. Identify the Profiles

- Use the wheel to locate the dominant flavor(s) of your bourbon (sweet, spicy, woody, fruity).
- Then do the same for your cigar (earthy, sweet, spicy, herbal).

### 2. Choose a Strategy

- Complementary (green): Match similar notes (e.g., vanilla & cream).
- Contrasting (red): Pair opposites (e.g., spicy rye & creamy cigar).
- Balanced (yellow): Find harmony between mild intensity and flavor contrast.

### 3. Adjust for Balance

- Light bourbons go best with milder cigars.
- High-proof bourbons can overwhelm—add water to soften or pair with a bolder cigar.

## Quick Pairing Examples

🟢 *Complementary*: Wheated Bourbon + Connecticut Shade — Sweet and creamy on both sides, this pairing delivers buttery smoothness.

🔴 *Contrasting*: Rye Bourbon + Nicaraguan Cigar — Bold spice meets earthy power in a dynamic match.

🟡 *Balanced*: Sherry-Finished Bourbon + Maduro — Rich fruit notes align with cocoa and leather for layered depth.

With this tool, pairing moves from guesswork to guided discovery, helping you craft matches that satisfy the palate and celebrate the craft.

# Bourbon & Cigar Pairing Wheel

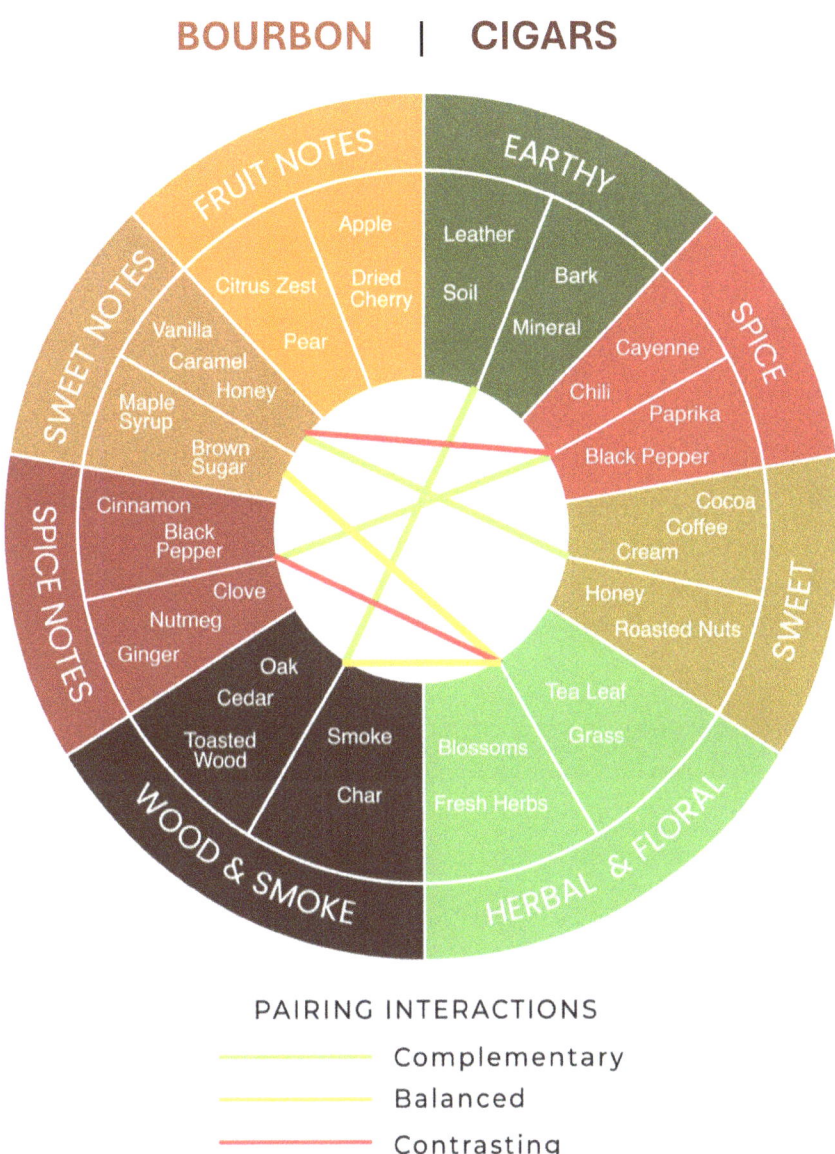

155

# III. Practical Tips for Pairing

Crafting a great bourbon and cigar pairing requires attention to preparation, mindfulness, and exploration. From cleansing the palate to documenting preferences and embracing experimentation, these strategies help enthusiasts deepen their appreciation and refine their pairing skills.

## Palate Preparation & Progression

A successful pairing begins with a clean palate and a thoughtful progression. Sparkling water or unsalted crackers help clear lingering flavors, while structured tasting—starting with mild and moving to bold—prepares the senses for complexity.

Begin with a smooth wheated bourbon and a Connecticut Shade cigar, then advance to a mid-proof bourbon with a medium-bodied cigar. Finish with a high-proof rye and a bold Maduro. This sequence lets each pairing build on the last, creating a more enjoyable and coherent experience.

## Recording Your Experience

Taking notes during tastings helps you track what works—and why. You should record:
- Bourbon: Brand, proof, age, and any barrel finish
- Cigar: Brand, wrapper, body (mild, medium, full)
- Flavors: Key tasting notes and how they interacted
- Impressions: Balance? Overpowering? Surprising synergy?

*For example: "Bourbon: Pappy Van Winkle 15-Year, 107 proof. Cigar: Padron 1964 Anniversary, Maduro. Flavors: Bourbon's caramel and dried cherry; cigar's cocoa and pepper; together, the cigar's earth softened the bourbon's sweetness. Impression: Balanced — neither overwhelmed the other."*

Over time, your notes become a personal pairing guide—and a great way to share favorites with fellow enthusiasts.

### Experimentation & Innovation

The most memorable pairings often come from experimentation. Don't be afraid to go off-script. Try mixing bolder bourbons with milder cigars, or flipping that dynamic. Explore new barrel finishes, like rum or toasted oak, and see how they interact with earthy or smoky tobaccos.

Try sequential pairings: same cigar, different bourbons—or vice versa. Compare, contrast, and refine. The more you test combinations, the more confident and intuitive your pairing skills will become.

Innovation isn't about breaking rules. It's about discovering new dimensions of flavor, one pairing at a time.

## Conclusion: Curating the Experience

Pairing bourbon and cigars is more than matching flavors. It's about crafting an experience. The key lies in understanding how grain recipes, barrel aging, and proof levels shape bourbon, and how those elements interact with cigar strength, body, and character.

But knowledge alone isn't enough. Great pairings come from exploration. Guidelines help—but the most memorable combinations often come from curiosity, trial, and instinct. As your palate evolves, so too will your preferences. The pairing that feels perfect today may open the door to something even better tomorrow.

Bourbon and cigars are both living crafts—rooted in heritage, yet always moving forward. The best pairings reflect that same spirit: grounded in tradition, open to discovery.

In the next chapter, *The Art of Tasting & Pairing Like a Pro*, we'll bring it all together—transforming insight into practice, and turning every pairing into a ritual worth savoring.

# CHAPTER 10

# The Art of Tasting & Pairing Like a Pro

Pairing bourbon and cigars is more than an indulgence. It's a deliberate ritual that blends tradition, chemistry, and personal expression. When done well, a pairing creates a layered experience that engages the senses and honors the craftsmanship behind both bourbon and cigars.

This chapter draws together insights from earlier sections to offer a practical framework for pairing with purpose. Whether guided by cultural appreciation, scientific understanding, or personal intuition, the goal is the same: to heighten enjoyment through mindful engagement.

The chapter is structured in three parts:
- Preparation explores how to set the stage, from ambiance and tools to palate cleansing.
- Technique covers tasting strategies like nosing, sipping, and retrohaling.
- Reflection offers ways to document preferences and develop a personal pairing style.

Armed with these tools, you'll be able to pair with greater confidence, depth, and intentionality, transforming simple indulgence into elevated practice.

# I. Preparation: Setting the Stage for Pairing

A memorable pairing begins long before the first sip or draw. The environment, the tools, and the readiness of your palate all shape how flavor unfolds. Attending to these elements turns tasting into a mindful ritual, one that respects both the moment and the materials.

## Creating the Ideal Environment

Ambiance influences perception. A calm, uncluttered setting helps you focus on aroma, texture, and flavor. Warm, dim lighting encourages relaxation, while moderate room temperature preserves the subtleties of both spirit and smoke. Heat can make bourbon feel aggressive and cause cigars to burn too quickly; cold can mute complexity.

Avoid overpowering scents like perfume, air fresheners, or food aromas, which interfere with flavor. Even ambient noise or distraction can diminish the experience. The goal is to create a neutral, attentive space, an atmosphere that lets the pairing speak.

## Tools of the Trade

Thoughtful preparation begins with the right equipment. Each tool enhances either precision or pleasure.

*Cigar Essentials*

- **Cutters:** Straight cuts offer an open draw; V-cuts intensify flavor by concentrating smoke; punch cuts create a more controlled experience. Choose based on the cigar's shape and your preferred resistance.
- **Lighters:** Butane torch lighters are clean and efficient. For a more

ceremonial feel, cedar spills or long wooden matches add traditional flair.

- **Ashtrays:** A stable, well-designed ashtray supports the cigar without disrupting the burn and completes the visual setting.

*Glassware for Bourbon*

- **Tulip Glasses:** Narrow openings focus the nose—ideal for high-proof or aromatic bourbons.
- **Glencairn Glasses:** The tasting standard, engineered to reveal layers of aroma and texture.
- **Whiskey Tumblers:** Less focused, but tactile and approachable, ideal for relaxed settings.

Together, these elements help signal that you're not simply consuming. You're curating.

## Palate Preparation

Your palate is the medium on which flavor is painted. Preparing it well ensures that both the bourbon and cigar can express their full character.

*Cleanse the Palate*

Remove lingering flavors from food, drink, or earlier cigars:
- **Still Water:** Hydrates and clears the mouth.
- **Sparkling Water:** Bubbles help remove oils and heavy flavors.
- **Plain Crackers or Bread:** Neutral reset without interference.

*Plan the Sequence*

Treat the session like a tasting flight:
- **Bourbon:** Start with lighter styles—wheated or lower-proof expressions—then progress to spicier or barrel-strength pours.
- **Cigars:** Begin with Connecticut Shade or light-bodied blends, then move to medium and full-bodied smokes like Maduro.

Pacing matters. A mindful sequence lets each pairing shine and transforms the session into a journey.

## II. Technique: The Tasting Process

Pairing bourbon and cigars is not a casual indulgence. It's a sensory ritual rooted in patience, precision, and awareness. Mastering the techniques of tasting elevates each sip and draw into a layered experience where aroma, flavor, and texture converge. This section explores how to taste both cigars and bourbon, and how to bring them into dialogue through thoughtful pairing.

### Cigar Tasting: Drawing Out the Flavor

The journey begins with the cigar. Every detail—from how it's cut and lit to how the smoke is drawn—affects its flavor profile and how it interacts with bourbon.

*Cutting and Lighting*

A proper cut ensures a smooth draw and even burn:
- **Straight cuts** offer a classic, open draw.
- **V-cuts** concentrate smoke and amplify flavor.
- **Punch cuts** create a tighter draw and focused intensity.

Lighting matters just as much. A slow, even toast of the foot with a butane torch ensures balance. Wooden matches or cedar spills add a touch of tradition, making the lighting process feel ceremonial.

*Drawing, Retrohaling, and Evaluating Flavor*

Drawing is about savoring, not inhaling. A slow, steady pull coats the palate and releases layers of complexity.

**Retrohaling**—gently exhaling smoke through the nose—activates olfactory receptors, unlocking hidden notes like spice, cocoa, florals, and earth. It's one of the most effective ways to deepen your understanding of a cigar's character.

As the cigar burns, flavors evolve. Strength, sweetness, or spice may rise or recede. Pay attention to these transitions—they're the heartbeat of the experience.

### Recognizing Tasting Notes

While subjective, cigar flavors often fall into broad categories:
- **Spice:** Black pepper, cinnamon, clove
- **Cream:** Buttery textures, often found in Connecticut Shade wrappers
- **Earth:** Soil, leather, oak; common in Broadleaf and Maduro
- **Sweetness:** Cocoa, dried fruit, honey; especially in aged cigars

Identifying these components is key to selecting a bourbon that either complements or contrasts effectively.

## Bourbon Tasting: The Art of Sipping & Nosing

If the cigar offers a slow burn of evolving character, bourbon delivers a layered cascade of aromas, warmth, and flavor, best appreciated through careful nosing and sipping.

### Nosing: Discovering Aromas

Use a tulip or Glencairn glass to concentrate the bourbon's bouquet. Start by holding the glass slightly away from your nose to pick up lighter top notes, then draw closer to explore deeper layers.

Common aromatic profiles include:
- **Vanilla & Caramel:** From oak barrel lignin
- **Spice:** Rye grain or barrel char may yield cinnamon, clove, or pepper
- **Fruit & Floral:** Esters can evoke apple, pear, banana, or honey

- **Oak & Smoke:** From aging and char level

These scents are more than prelude. They often mirror what unfolds on the palate.

*Sipping: Letting Flavor Unfold*

Sip slowly and allow the bourbon to rest on your tongue. The typical arc begins with sweetness, followed by spice, fruit, or wood, and ends with a warm, lingering finish.

*Mouthfeel and Finish*

Texture matters. High-proof bourbons tend to feel richer and heavier, ideal for full-bodied cigars. Lower-proof or wheated bourbons are softer, matching better with delicate blends.

The finish—how long flavors linger—affects pairing. A long, complex finish pairs well with robust cigars; a clean, short finish may be better suited for milder blends.

## The Pairing Process: Creating Sensory Harmony

Once you've tasted each element on its own, the true art of pairing begins through contrast, complement, or balance.

*Alternate Sip and Draw*

Alternate slowly between a puff and a sip. Let the cigar smoke linger on the palate before tasting the bourbon. This creates a sensory bridge where each enhances the other.

Complement, Contrast, Balance:
- **Complement:** A bourbon with caramel and vanilla aligns beautifully with a cocoa-laced Maduro.
- **Contrast:** A spicy rye bourbon cuts through a creamy Connecticut

cigar for a lively counterpoint.
- **Balance:** A slightly sweet cigar might temper a sharp bourbon, creating harmony.

### Adjusting the Experience

Fine-tune as needed. A splash of water in the bourbon softens intensity. Waiting between draws gives a bold cigar time to cool. Adjusting tempo and strength lets you tailor the pairing to your palate.

The tasting process is where knowledge becomes experience. By learning to read both cigar and bourbon through scent, flavor, and feel, you gain not only greater control but greater pleasure. The final step lies in reflection, where technique turns into personal style.

# III. Reflection: Documenting and Refining Your Pairings

Pairing bourbon and cigars is a journey of refinement—equal parts exploration and self-discovery. The more intentionally you approach each experience, the more your palate evolves. Through consistent reflection and note-taking, casual enjoyment becomes craft. This section offers tools for deepening your understanding, developing your own pairing style, and curating experiences with purpose.

### Keeping Notes: Capturing the Experience

Every pairing is an opportunity to learn. Whether using a leather-bound journal or a tasting app, consistency is key. The goal is to preserve the memory—not just what you enjoyed, but why it worked.

Core elements to record:
- **Cigar:** Brand, wrapper, origin, and strength (mild, medium, full)
- **Bourbon:** Brand, proof, mash bill (if known), barrel finish, and age
- **Flavors:** Tasting notes from both cigar and bourbon
- **Interaction:** Complementary, contrasting, or balanced?

- **Impression:** Would you revisit the pairing? What stood out?

## Creating Your Tasting Journal

You don't need a formal template. Just a repeatable system that helps you track what matters. A simple grid or sectioned note with categories for strength, flavor notes, balance, surprises, and overall impression will do. Over time, your journal becomes a personal flavor map—and a powerful tool for growth.

Bonus: Sharing your notes with others—at lounges, tasting events, or online—invites conversation and sparks new ideas.

## Refining Your Palate: Building a Flavor Library

Beyond logging experiences, your notes form the basis of a personal flavor library, a mental catalogue of what your palate prefers. Patterns will emerge.

You may find that:
- Wheated bourbons shine with creamy Connecticut Shade cigars
- Spicy ryes pair best with bold, peppery Nicaraguans
- Port- or sherry-finished bourbons elevate rich Maduros

These insights not only guide future pairings; they inspire new ones.

## Developing a Personal Pairing Philosophy

As your preferences take shape, so does your philosophy. Some gravitate toward balance, others thrive on contrast. Maybe you seek symmetry between smoke and spirit, or delight in the tension where opposites meet. Your pairing style becomes a reflection of your taste, temperament, and curiosity. The point isn't to follow rules. It's to discover what brings you the most satisfaction and to keep exploring from there.

## Crafting Signature Pairings: The Art of Curating Experiences

With time and experience, pairing evolves into curation. You're no longer just matching flavors. You're shaping a mood, an atmosphere, a memory.

A signature pairing is more than the right bourbon and cigar. It's the intentional orchestration of moment, setting, and feeling.

Try building a themed tasting flight:
- **Bold & Spicy:** A Nicaraguan cigar with a high-proof rye, crackling with pepper and fire
- **Soft & Sweet:** A creamy Connecticut Shade with a vanilla-rich wheated bourbon

Think of it like a tasting menu: light selections first, building gradually toward bolder expressions. The arc of the session becomes a story told in smoke and sip.

Ambiance matters. Warm light, thoughtful music, elegant tools all contribute to the ritual. A quiet night with a jazz record and single pairing can be meditative. A well-curated evening with friends becomes celebration.

### Final Reflection

Your pairings will come to express more than taste. They'll embody your style, your values, your way of savoring. They represent a deepening relationship with two crafts that reward attention, intention, and time. In reflection, pairing finds its deeper purpose.

# IV. Practical Pairing Guides & Recommendations

The art of pairing comes alive when theory meets experience. Now that you've explored flavor science, technique, and ritual, this section offers a set of thoughtfully curated combinations to guide your next tasting session.

These aren't fixed formulas. They're invitations to experiment, refine, and develop your own pairing instincts.

Rather than organizing by specific distilleries or cigar brands (as the: *Bourbon & Cigar Pairing Guide by Distillery* does), these recommendations are grouped by *experience level* and *flavor themes*, offering a flexible framework to grow your confidence and creativity.

## 🟢 Beginner Pairings: Start Smooth

For newcomers, the goal is to build comfort and palate awareness. The best pairings here emphasize balance, smoothness, and approachability.

- **Flavor Strategy:** Match mild cigars (e.g., Connecticut Shade) with softer, wheated bourbons or 90-proof classics.
- **Why It Works:** These combinations allow subtle notes to shine without overwhelming the senses. Focus on creamy, woody, or slightly sweet interactions.

*Example Flavor Themes:*
- Vanilla + Cedar
- Caramel + Toasted Almond
- Light Spice + Cream

## 🟡 Intermediate Pairings: Embrace Complexity

As your confidence grows, it's time to explore more dynamic flavor interactions—layered spice, bolder wrappers, and unique barrel finishes.

- **Flavor Strategy:** Try pairing high-rye bourbons or double-oaked expressions with medium- to full-bodied cigars like Sungrown (sun-cured wrappers with deep, robust flavor) or Maduro.
- **Why It Works:** These pairings introduce contrast, where sweetness offsets spice or fruit balances earth.

*Example Flavor Themes:*
- Stone Fruit + Cocoa
- Rye Spice + Maduro Earth
- Nutmeg + Espresso

## 🔴 Advanced Pairings: Bold & Intense

At this level, the focus is on high-proof bourbons, powerful cigars, and rich, lingering finishes. These combinations demand attention and reward patience.

- **Flavor Strategy:** Combine barrel-proof bourbons with bold Nicaraguan cigars or fire-cured tobaccos. Look for complexity, structure, and evolving layers.
- **Why It Works:** Strong profiles challenge and refine the palate. Each sip and draw becomes a conversation of deep flavors.

*Example Flavor Themes:*
- Char + Black Pepper
- Dark Fruit + Leather
- Caramelized Oak + Spice Bomb

## 🌟 Seasonal & Creative Pairings: Explore the Unexpected

Some of the most memorable pairings come from playful experimentation and attention to mood, season, or even setting.

- **Spring & Summer:** Light, floral bourbons with creamy, aromatic cigars.
- **Autumn & Winter:** Heavier, oak-laden bourbons with earthy Broadleaf cigars or fire-cured selections.
- **Creative Themes:** Try port-finished bourbons with chocolate-forward cigars, or experiment with niche options like tea-infused wrappers paired with spicy ryes.

*Example Flavor Themes:*
- Fig + Charred Oak (Fall)
- Lemon Zest + White Pepper (Spring)
- Cinnamon + Toasted Walnut (Holiday Pairings)

Whatever your experience level, the goal is the same: create a pairing that invites attention, enjoyment, and reflection. Let flavor lead the way, but stay open to surprises.

> For additional distillery-based recommendations and pairing suggestions, see: *Bourbon & Cigar Pairing Guide by Distillery* (page 182).

## Conclusion: The Endless Journey of Pairing

Pairing bourbon and cigars is more than a pastime. It is a ritual that fuses history, culture, chemistry, and creativity. This chapter has offered the tools and insights needed to approach pairings with confidence, intention, and a spirit of discovery.

Throughout this journey, three themes have emerged. First, knowledge lays the foundation. Understanding mash bills, barrel aging, proof, and finishing—and how these elements interact with the world of cigars— enables you to create pairings that are not just harmonious, but transformative.

Second, technique shapes the experience. From nosing a bourbon to retrohaling a cigar, method matters. The right glassware, pacing, and ambiance turn an ordinary moment into something immersive and memorable.

Finally, personal expression brings it all to life. The most meaningful pairings don't follow rules—they follow curiosity. Whether it's the silkiness of a wheated bourbon with a creamy Connecticut Shade, or the bold crackle of a high-proof rye with a peppery Nicaraguan, the magic lies in the pursuit.

Even with all this guidance, the journey is far from over. Pairing is a living art, shaped by changing tastes, seasonal releases, and the evolving refinement of your own palate. The "perfect" pairing is never final; it is rediscovered with every pour, every spark, every note on the tongue.

In the next and final section of this book, we'll pull together the full story, from heritage and chemistry to craft and culture, and celebrate the enduring legacy of bourbon and cigars as America's most iconic and expressive indulgences.

# CONCLUSION

# The Enduring Legacy of Bourbon & Cigars

As we close these pages, we're left with more than a deeper appreciation for bourbon and cigars. We're left with a story—a living narrative of resilience, ingenuity, and the timeless pursuit of craftsmanship. These two traditions, born from the resourcefulness of colonial America and shaped through centuries of adversity and innovation, stand today as enduring symbols of persistence, creativity, and cultural pride.

From their origins as economic staples that fueled early commerce, bourbon and cigars rose to become markers of identity and refinement. In the 19th century, they found a place in private clubs, grand salons, and celebratory rituals—not just as luxuries, but as handcrafted statements of quality and tradition. Their appeal was never rooted solely in wealth, but in the artistry that set them apart from the ordinary.

The 20th century tested these traditions. Prohibition, the Great Depression, the Cuban Embargo, and sweeping cultural shifts might have extinguished them. But bourbon and cigars endured. Through mass production and corporate consolidation, they bent without breaking.

Devoted artisans and loyal enthusiasts kept the flame alive, insisting that authenticity mattered, even when convenience and conformity reigned.

The revival that began in the 1980s and blossomed in the 1990s was more than a market resurgence—it was a reclamation. Bourbon's renaissance, led by visionaries like Julian Van Winkle III, Elmer T. Lee, and Booker Noe, proved that small-batch and single-barrel quality could triumph over mass production. Meanwhile, the cigar world reinvented itself, transforming Nicaragua, the Dominican Republic, and Honduras into new epicenters of excellence, redefining what it meant to create a world-class cigar.

The 1990s cigar boom underscored what bourbon had also proven: that when culture rediscovers craft, passion and innovation follow. Boutique cigar makers experimented with blends and fermentation; bourbon distillers returned to traditional methods with renewed vigor. Innovation was no longer about novelty. It was about depth, character, and honoring the past while forging the future.

But as we've explored, bourbon and cigars are not just parallel stories. They are intertwined—chemically, sensorially, even spiritually. Their pairing is more than coincidence. Phenolic compounds, esters, terpenes, and ethanol create interactions that are scientifically fascinating, and yet, the pleasure they offer together transcends science. There is chemistry, yes—but there is also magic.

Geography and terroir play their part. The limestone-rich water of Kentucky and the volcanic soil of Estelí are not romantic abstractions. They are the essence of what makes bourbon and cigars taste like no other indulgence. Understanding this connection to land and labor deepens the experience, inviting us to see pairing as an act of reverence as much as enjoyment.

The most meaningful pairings arise from a blend of knowledge, technique, and personal expression. Whether you seek complementary harmony, bold contrast, or subtle balance, the goal is not perfection—but presence. The best pairings are those that invite you to slow down, pay attention, and truly savor the moment.

Today's resurgence of bourbon and cigars is not just cultural nostalgia—it is a renaissance of meaning. In an age of speed and disposability, they offer a reminder that craftsmanship, connection, and ritual still matter. They ask us to be deliberate. To be curious. To create space for reflection and pleasure, whether alone with our thoughts or in the company of others.

Looking ahead, bourbon and cigars will continue to evolve. New techniques, barrel finishes, fermentation processes, and varietals will shape the next chapter. But their heart will remain unchanged. They will continue to bring us moments of joy and contemplation—moments that speak to something deeper than taste.

And ultimately, that may be their greatest gift. For all the science and culture, pairing bourbon and cigars is about joy. It is about celebrating life's finer moments—crafted with care, shared with purpose, and remembered not just for how they tasted, but for how they made us feel.

The art of pairing, in the end, is the art of being present. It's the quiet luxury of intention. The joy of tradition reborn. The creation of something extraordinary, one sip and one draw at a time.

# Glossary of Key Terms

## Cigar-Specific Terms

**Binder** - The tobacco leaf that holds the filler tobacco together in a cigar. The binder helps shape the cigar and influences its burn and flavor.

**Cap** - The small piece of wrapper leaf applied to the head of a cigar, which must be cut before smoking.

**Cedar Aging** - The practice of aging cigars in a cedar-lined room to impart woody or earthy tones.

**Draw** - The resistance felt when puffing on a cigar. A good draw provides an easy and smooth smoke.

**Filler** - The innermost tobacco leaves that form the core of a cigar, responsible for the majority of its flavor and burning characteristics.

**Humidor** - A climate-controlled container or room designed to maintain ideal humidity levels for storing cigars.

**Ligero** - A type of tobacco leaf found at the top of the tobacco plant, known for its strength and bold flavor.

**Maduro** - A term used for cigars made from tobacco aged longer, resulting in darker wrappers that provide deeper, sweeter flavors.

**Plume (or Bloom)** - A harmless crystallization of oils on the surface of a cigar, indicating age and proper storage—not to be confused with mold.

**Retrohaling** - The practice of drawing cigar smoke through the nose after inhaling it through the mouth to enhance the tasting experience.

**Ring Gauge** - A measurement of a cigar's diameter, with each unit representing 1/64 of an inch. Helps determine the cigar's size and potential flavor intensity.

**Seco** - A type of tobacco leaf from the lower part of the tobacco plant, known for its milder flavor and contribution to a cigar's overall balance.

**Toasting** - The act of gently warming the foot of a cigar with a flame before lighting, to ensure an even burn.

**Wrapper** - The outermost tobacco leaf that covers the cigar. It is the most influential on the cigar's flavor and appearance.

**Wrapper Leaf** - The outer leaf of a cigar that affects both the look and taste of the cigar. Typically shade-grown for smoother texture.

**Viso** - A type of tobacco leaf located in the middle of the plant. It is known for being more balanced in flavor and strength compared to Ligero and Seco.

**Vitola** - The specific size and shape of a cigar, which can influence its smoking characteristics and flavor profile.

## Bourbon-Specific Terms

**Angel's Share** – The portion of bourbon that evaporates during barrel aging, often cited as a romantic metaphor for the spirit lost to time and nature.

**Barrel Finishing** - Aging bourbon in barrels previously used to store other liquids like sherry or rum to impart unique flavors.

**Bottled-in-Bond** - A designation for bourbon that meets specific legal requirements including being produced by one distiller in a single season, aged at least four years, and bottled at 100 proof.

**Bourbon** - An American whiskey made from at least 51% corn, aged in new charred oak barrels.

**Cask Strength** - Bourbon bottled directly from the barrel without dilution, resulting in higher ABV and robust flavor.

**Charred Oak Barrels** - Burned oak barrels that impart vanilla, caramel, and smoke flavors during bourbon aging.

**Cooperage** – A facility or workshop where barrels are crafted; also refers to the craft of barrel-making.

**High-Rye Bourbon** – A bourbon with a higher-than-average percentage of rye in the mash bill, resulting in bolder spice and heat.

**Mash Bill** - The recipe used to make bourbon, consisting of a combination of grains such as corn, rye, wheat, and barley.

**Proof** - A measurement of alcohol content; one proof equals 2% alcohol by volume.

**Rye Bourbon** - Bourbon made with at least 51% rye, producing a spicier, more peppery flavor profile.

**Sour Mash** – A distilling technique that uses a portion of a previous fermentation batch to start a new one, helping maintain consistency and pH.

**Straight Bourbon** - Bourbon that has been aged for at least two years and contains no added coloring or flavoring.

**Tennessee Whiskey** – A type of bourbon produced in Tennessee that undergoes the Lincoln County Process (charcoal filtering) before aging; meets all federal requirements for bourbon but is branded differently.

**Wheated Bourbon** - Bourbon made with at least 51% corn and a significant amount of wheat for a smoother, sweeter flavor profile.

## Pairing & Sensory Related Terms

**Complementary Pairing** - Matching bourbon and cigar flavors that share similar notes to reinforce a sensory theme.

**Contrasting Pairing** - Combining bourbon and cigar profiles with opposing flavors (e.g., sweet vs. spicy) to highlight complexity and tension.

**Balance** - A pairing strategy where no one element overpowers the other; harmony across flavor, intensity, and duration.

**Cross-Modal Perception** - The brain's ability to combine multiple sensory inputs (e.g., taste, smell, texture) into a unified flavor experience.

**Cigars & Bourbon Pairing** - The art of combining bourbon with a specific cigar to enhance the sensory experience.

**Finish** - The lingering flavors and sensations after tasting bourbon or smoking a cigar.

**Flavor Profile** - The combination of flavors and aromas detected in both cigars and bourbon.

**Mouthfeel** - The physical sensation and texture of bourbon or cigar smoke in the mouth.

**Pairing** - The process of matching bourbon with cigars to enhance the flavor experience.

**Palate Cleansing** - The process of neutralizing taste buds between tastings.

**Smoke** - The vapor that is exhaled after a puff on a cigar or released during bourbon aging.

**Super Tasting** - A term for individuals with heightened sensitivity to flavors.

**Tasting Notes** - Descriptive terms used to characterize the sensory experience of tasting a cigar or bourbon.

**Terroir** - Regional characteristics like soil, climate, and geography influencing the flavor of bourbon and cigars.

## Technical/Scientific Terms

**Aldehydes** - Compounds formed during fermentation and aging that contribute to aroma and flavor.

**Esters** - Aromatic compounds formed during fermentation and aging that contribute fruity or floral notes to both bourbon and cigars.

**Fermentation** - The process of breaking down sugars to develop flavor in cigars and convert sugars to alcohol in bourbon.

**Fusel Oils** - Complex alcohols produced during fermentation that impact bourbon's flavor profile.

**Phenolic Compounds** - Organic molecules that contribute to bitterness, smokiness, and astringency.

**Tannins** - Naturally occurring compounds from wood or tobacco that add astringency or dryness to the mouthfeel.

**Terpenes** - Organic compounds that contribute to the aroma and flavor of tobacco and bourbon, often associated with citrus, pine, or floral notes.

# Appendix: Bourbon & Cigar Pairing Guide by Distillery

This appendix offers a practical companion to *Smoke & Oak* by matching 30 prominent American distilleries—20 from Kentucky and 10 from Tennessee—with cigar pairings that reflect each bourbon's character, flavor profile, and historical or cultural resonance. While many pairing guides focus on tasting notes alone, this one also honors the craft traditions, heritage, and regional nuance that shape each distillery's identity.

---

## Kentucky Pride, Tennessee Legacy — Why Both Belong

**Why include Tennessee whiskeys?**[17] While Kentucky is widely celebrated as bourbon's heartland, Tennessee's distilling heritage runs just as deep. Iconic brands like *Jack Daniel's* and *Uncle Nearest* are not only historically significant but also central to the broader American whiskey tradition. Their inclusion in this guide reflects a key principle of pairing: flavor—not geography—should lead.

By federal production standards, most Tennessee whiskeys meet every requirement for bourbon— 51%+ corn, new charred oak barrels, proof limits—and could legally be labeled "bourbon" if their producers chose. However, since 2013, Tennessee state law requires "Tennessee whiskey" to also undergo the Lincoln County Process, a maple-charcoal filtration step before barreling. Most producers embrace this designation as a marker of regional craft. In short, Tennessee whiskey shares bourbon's foundation while adding a defining production step of its own.

Of course, some Kentucky bourbon purists might disagree. Many believe that *true* bourbon can only come from Kentucky, citing the state's limestone water, seasonal climate, and centuries of expertise as defining features. While their pride is justified— Kentucky does produce over 90% of the world's bourbon—federal standards say otherwise.

This guide honors both perspectives: it respects the heritage of Kentucky bourbon while acknowledging that great whiskey is made in more than one place. When it comes to pairing, let taste—not labels—do the talking.

---

[17]According to the Kentucky Distillers' Association, Kentucky is responsible for approximately 95% of the world's bourbon — meaning whiskey labeled and produced as Kentucky bourbon. Some industry observers note that this figure shifts to roughly 75% if Tennessee whiskey (a bourbon-style spirit produced under different state law) is counted. In 2023, Tennessee led all states in total distilled spirits exports at $983 million—driven largely by Jack Daniel's Tennessee whiskey—followed by Kentucky at $505 million, primarily bourbon. Some Tennessee distillers (such as Chattanooga Whiskey) produce spirits that meet all federal bourbon standards and label them as bourbon, since their products do not undergo the Lincoln County Process required for Tennessee whiskey designation. Sources: Kentucky Distillers' Association; Distilled Spirits Council of the United States, *American Spirits Export Report 2023*.

These pairings are not meant to be prescriptive or exhaustive. Rather, they provide starting points—grounded in both sensory logic and historical affinity—for enthusiasts seeking to explore meaningful connections between spirit and cigar. Some brands are paired with *Antebellum* cigars to evoke historically informed American blends, while others feature celebrated boutique cigars to ensure variety and avoid promotional bias.

Whether you're visiting a distillery, curating a tasting experience, or simply enjoying a quiet evening with a pour and a draw, this guide is designed to help you pair with purpose—and pleasure.

*Note: Several distilleries in this guide are based in Tennessee but produce whiskeys other than "Tennessee whiskey" in the legal sense. Tennessee whiskey, by state law, requires the Lincoln County Process (maple-charcoal filtration before barreling). Some Tennessee distilleries — including Chattanooga Whiskey and Corsair — produce bourbon, single malt, rye, or other American whiskey styles distilled in Tennessee. These are noted in their respective entries.*

1. **Buffalo Trace Distillery (Frankfort)**
   Buffalo Trace's signature bourbon—known for its rich caramel, toffee, and vanilla notes—calls for a pairing that can match both its depth and balance. The *Antebellum No. 1 – The Colonel* (Medium-to-Strong Blend) brings an earthy, cocoa-driven profile that complements the bourbon's oak and spice with historical resonance and complexity.
   **Alternative pairing:** Try the *Padron 2000 Maduro*, whose bold Nicaraguan character adds a peppery layer that plays beautifully against Buffalo Trace's smooth finish.

2. **Maker's Mark (Loretto)**
   Maker's wheated mash bill yields a soft, sweet bourbon with notes of red fruit, vanilla, and toasted oak. A mild-to-medium cigar works best here. The *Arturo Fuente Hemingway Signature*, with its creamy Dominican blend and delicate cedar undertones, mirrors the bourbon's elegance.
   **Historical pairing option:** The *Antebellum No. 2 – The Statesman* (Light-to-Medium Blend) offers a balanced touch of wood, subtle cocoa, and mild sweetness—evoking the refinement of pre-war tobacco craft and echoing Maker's smooth profile.

3. **Jim Beam American Stillhouse (Clermont)**

Jim Beam's classic bourbon leans into toasted oak, spice, and nutty vanilla— a solid backbone for a cigar with presence. The *Oliva Serie V Melanio Maduro* pairs exceptionally well, delivering rich chocolate and pepper without overwhelming the palate.

**For an American heritage experience:** The *Antebellum No. 1 – The Colonel* adds structured strength and depth, echoing the bourbon's intensity with a historical nod to 19th-century cigar traditions.

4. **Woodford Reserve (Versailles)**

Woodford Reserve's balanced and complex profile—with its layers of dried fruit, toasted oak, and spice—invites a refined cigar companion. The *Antebellum No. 2 – The Statesman* (Light-to-Medium Blend) is a superb match, offering a smooth, nuanced smoke with notes of cream, light wood, and cocoa that complement the bourbon's finesse. For those who prefer a contemporary touch, try the *Perdomo Reserve Champagne*—its mild sweetness and creamy texture echo the bourbon's round finish.

---

### How Distillery Meets Cigar

Each cigar selection in this guide is designed to complement its corresponding bourbon not only in flavor, but also in body, texture, and historical resonance. These criteria guide every recommendation:

#### 1. Flavor Synergy
Bourbons rich in caramel, spice, oak, or fruit are paired with cigars that echo or elevate those notes. Cocoa meets charred oak, pepper plays off rye spice—each pairing is tuned to harmonize or contrast with purpose.

#### 2. Body and Balance
No mismatched intensities here. Lighter-bodied whiskeys (e.g., Castle & Key, Sugarlands) are paired with smoother smokes like the Avo or Arturo Fuente Hemingway. Bolder bourbons (e.g., Bulleit, Corsair) meet their match in full-bodied cigars like Padron, Alec Bradley, or E.P. Carrillo.

#### 3. Aromatic & Textural Coherence
Subtle aromas—leather, nuttiness, floral tones—find their counterpart in the cigar. This layered coherence is especially evident in whiskeys with unique finishes, like Angel's Envy or Chattanooga's Experimental Series.

#### 4. Historical & Cultural Framing
Some pairings reach beyond taste. Antebellum cigars are selected not just for their profiles but for their thematic fit—honoring stories like J.W. Kelly's tobacconist heritage or Leiper's Fork's Bottled-in-Bond legacy.

---

5. **Heaven Hill Bourbon Experience (Bardstown)**

Heaven Hill's classic bourbons tend to feature rich caramel, vanilla, and baking spice notes with a warm oak backbone. These qualities pair wonderfully with the bold, earthy character of the *Antebellum No. 1 – The Colonel* (Medium-to-Strong Blend), which brings dark cocoa and subtle spice to the table. Alternatively, the *Alec Bradley Prensado* offers a similarly bold experience with a slightly more peppery profile—ideal for those wanting to intensify the interplay of flavors.

6. **Wild Turkey Distillery (Lawrenceburg)**

Wild Turkey's bold bourbon delivers spice, charred oak, and deep caramel, thanks to a bourbon profile aged longer than most and entered into the barrel at lower proof. A great match is the *La Aroma de Cuba Mi Amor*, a medium-to-full-bodied cigar that introduces espresso and pepper to echo the bourbon's intensity. For a historical nod, the *Antebellum No. 1 – The Colonel* provides a strong, earthy profile rooted in pre-Civil War tobacco, adding depth and authenticity to this robust pairing.

7. **Bardstown Bourbon Company (Bardstown)**

Innovative and bold, Bardstown Bourbon Company blends tradition with modernity, producing complex bourbons with notes of spice, stone fruit, and toasted oak. A thoughtful companion to this profile is the *My Father Le Bijou 1922*—a rich Nicaraguan cigar that mirrors the bourbon's strength and sophistication. For a contemporary reflection of tradition and transformation, try *Exsul*—a Dominican puro composed of aged Cuban-seed tobaccos and rolled in the full *entubado* style. Its structured richness and elegant complexity mirror Bardstown's bold, layered bourbons while honoring the artistry of reinvention.

8. **Four Roses Distillery (Lawrenceburg)**

Known for its ten unique bourbon recipes and floral, fruity complexity, Four Roses pairs especially well with a lighter yet flavorful cigar. The *Antebellum No. 2 – The Statesman* (Light-to-Medium Blend) brings creamy notes of cocoa and subtle sweetness that accentuate the bourbon's nuanced bouquet. Another refined option is the *Oliva Serie V Melanio*, whose smooth chocolate and leather tones echo the bourbon's delicate spice and dried fruit finish.

### 9. Old Forester Distillery (Louisville)

As a staple of Louisville's Whiskey Row, Old Forester delivers a classic profile rich in caramel, oak, and baking spice. This timeless style is complemented by the *Antebellum No. 1 – The Colonel*, whose bold, earthy draw harmonizes with the bourbon's intensity. Alternatively, the *Punch Gran Puro* offers a spicy Honduran character that plays well with the bourbon's deep wood and pepper notes—an energetic pairing for the seasoned enthusiast.

### 10. Angel's Envy (Louisville)

A port barrel–finished bourbon from Angel's Envy reveals dark fruit, fig, and spice notes—an ideal match for a cigar with subtle sweetness and refined strength. Pair Angel's Envy with *Exsul*, a Dominican puro crafted entirely from Cuban-seed tobaccos and rolled using the traditional *entubado* technique. Its creamy cocoa, raisin-laced undertones, and balanced strength draw out the bourbon's port-rich finish, creating a pairing of quiet depth and lasting elegance. For a complementary alternative, try the *Oliva Serie V Melanio*, whose complexity mirrors the bourbon's elegance.

### 11. Lux Row Distillers (Bardstown)

Lux Row's bold, spice-forward bourbons benefit from an equally structured pairing. *Antebellum No. 1 – The Colonel* (Medium-to-Strong Blend) matches the bourbon's oak and clove intensity with its earthy depth and dark chocolate notes. If you prefer something with a Nicaraguan edge, consider the *Padron 1964 Anniversary Series*, which emphasizes toasted spice and a rich draw.

### 12. Willett Distillery (Bardstown)

Willett's small-batch bourbons often display vibrant spice and herbal layers. Pairing with *Antebellum No. 2 – The Statesman* allows a lighter-bodied experience that doesn't overpower the spirit's nuanced floral and citrus tones. For contrast, a *La Aroma de Cuba Mi Amor* cigar brings a mocha-sweetness and structured spice that can elevate the pairing into a balanced conversation of flavors.

### 13. Rabbit Hole Distillery (Louisville)

Known for its bold, modern bourbon profiles with toasted grain and cocoa notes, Rabbit Hole's signature expressions pair beautifully with cigars offering rich structure and earthy finish. *Antebellum No. 1 – The Colonel* brings dark cocoa and spice that resonate with the bourbon's warmth and depth. Alternatively, try the *My Father Le Bijou 1922*—a Nicaraguan powerhouse with similar boldness and layered spice.

## 14. Michter's Fort Nelson Distillery (Louisville)

Michter's elegant, spice-forward profile finds a compelling partner in *Exsul*—a Dominican puro made from Cuban-seed tobaccos and rolled in the meticulous *entubado* style. Its restrained richness and slow-building complexity echo the bourbon's quiet depth. It's a pairing of harmony and heritage. For a more pepper-forward contrast, the *Tatuaje Havana VI* offers red spice and leather, making for a refined yet expressive pairing.

## 15. Castle & Key Distillery (Frankfort)

With herbaceous, citrus-laced bourbon profiles, Castle & Key lends itself to pairings that favor finesse over brute strength. *Antebellum No. 2 – The Statesman* echoes this refinement with a creamy, gently aromatic profile. As a nuanced complement, consider the *Avo Classic No. 2*, a Dominican cigar that brings delicate floral notes and a clean finish, perfect for Castle & Key's botanical complexity.

## 16. Town Branch Distillery (Lexington)

Known for a bold, malty edge thanks to its brewing heritage, Town Branch bourbon benefits from a cigar that can match its toasty backbone. *Antebellum No. 1 – The Colonel* offers robust earth, cocoa, and spice—perfectly aligned with the bourbon's heavier oak and caramel notes. For an alternative, try the *La Aroma de Cuba Mi Amor*, which adds a chocolaty richness and subtle floral finish to round out the pairing.

## 17. Evan Williams Bourbon Experience (Louisville)

A classic bourbon with mass appeal and a smooth, vanilla-laced profile, Evan Williams shines when paired with a cigar that brings added structure without overwhelming. *Antebellum No. 1 – The Colonel* provides that strength and complementary flavor depth. Alternatively, the *Romeo y Julieta Reserva Real Nicaragua* offers cream and spice in a modern wrapper—balancing the bourbon's sweet oak charm with finesse.

18. **Green River Distilling Co. (Owensboro)**

With a flavor-forward profile featuring orchard fruit, oak, and toasted grain, Green River bourbon pairs beautifully with a cigar that offers both boldness and nuance. *Antebellum No. 2 – The Statesman* adds cream, soft cocoa, and light wood tones to mirror and soften the bourbon's fruit-spice balance. For contrast, the *Padron 2000 Maduro* introduces deeper pepper and espresso notes for a more intense ride.

19. **Wilderness Trail Distillery (Danville)**

Known for its scientific precision and respect for flavor nuance, Wilderness Trail bourbon often features layered sweetness, soft spice, and subtle complexity. *Antebellum No. 2 – The Statesman* enhances this profile with its creamy texture and delicate cocoa finish, preserving the bourbon's clarity while adding a whisper of rustic depth. For a bolder alternative, consider the *My Father Flor de Las Antillas*, whose nutmeg and cedar notes offer a refined counterpoint.

20. **Bulleit Distilling Co. (Shelbyville)**

With its high-rye mash bill, Bulleit bourbon delivers a sharp, spicy bite and lingering finish—traits that demand a cigar with backbone. *Antebellum No. 1 – The Colonel* rises to the occasion with bold earth, dark cocoa, and a structured burn that complements Bulleit's signature snap. Or opt for the *Oliva Serie V Melanio* for a more elegant take, bringing smooth espresso and spice to round out the rye's intensity.

21. **Jack Daniel's Distillery (Lynchburg) – *Tennessee Whiskey***

Tennessee whiskey's iconic charcoal mellowing process gives Jack Daniel's a smooth, slightly sweet character with banana, vanilla, and toasted oak. Pair it with *Antebellum No. 2 – The Statesman* for a gentle, harmonious experience where sweetness and earth meet in balance. For a refined twist, the *Avo XO Intermezzo* adds soft cream, nut, and subtle spice—drawing out the whiskey's quieter notes while enhancing its mellow charm.

22. **George Dickel Distillery (Tullahoma) – *Tennessee Whiskey***

Known for chilling its whiskey before maple-charcoal filtration—a distinctive twist on the Lincoln County Process—George Dickel leans toward smoothness with warm caramel, spice, and minerality. *Antebellum No. 2 – The*

*Statesman* provides a refined partner, echoing Dickel's mellow sweetness with creamy wood and subtle cocoa. For a deeper contrast, try the *E.P. Carrillo La Historia*, which layers rich espresso and spice against the whiskey's rounded finish.

### 23. **Nelson's Green Brier Distillery (Nashville) – *Tennessee Whiskey***

This revivalist distillery offers a bourbon that's balanced, floral, and slightly sweet—a nod to pre-Prohibition finesse. *Antebellum No. 2 – The Statesman* underscores its elegance, with light wood and aromatic leaf that keep the pairing clean and composed. Alternatively, the *La Aroma de Cuba Edición Especial* enhances the floral character while adding enough body to maintain interest through every sip.

### 24. **Uncle Nearest Premium Whiskey (Shelbyville) – *Tennessee Whiskey***

A Tennessee whiskey steeped in history and honor, Uncle Nearest's flagship expression is mellow yet complex, with brown sugar, vanilla, and gentle char. This calls for a cigar of subtle power—*My Father Connecticut* offers creamy notes and balanced spice that draw out the whiskey's depth without overpowering. For a historically grounded pairing, *Antebellum No. 1 – The Colonel* adds gravitas and structure, echoing the legacy the brand celebrates.

### 25. **Chattanooga Whiskey Experimental Distillery (Chattanooga) – *Tennessee Whiskey***

Founded with the Experimental Distillery in 2015 (the first distillery to make whiskey in Chattanooga in over 100 years), Chattanooga Whiskey has pioneered its own style: "Tennessee High Malt"—a straight bourbon distinguished by mash bills containing at least 25% specialty malted grains. The result is a richer, more malt-forward profile than typical bourbon, with notes of caramel, toasted grain, and chocolate. *Antebellum No. 2 – The Statesman* offers a fitting complement, with its light wood and subtle cocoa notes rounding out the malty complexity. For a more modern contrast, try the *Tatuaje Havana VI*, whose clean spice and structure add edge without overwhelming the pairing.

## 26. Corsair Distillery (Nashville) – *Tennessee Whiskey*

Founded in 2008, Corsair has built its reputation by pushing past the conventions of American whiskey, working with alternative grains, smoked malts, and unconventional techniques. Their flagship Triple Smoke—an American Single Malt made with cherrywood-, beechwood-, and peat-smoked barleys—earned Whisky Advocate's Artisan Whiskey of the Year and exemplifies the distillery's experimental ethos. Their Dark Rye and the new Tennessee Single Malt round out a whiskey lineup focused on layered, grain-forward complexity rather than traditional bourbon profiles. *Antebellum No. 1 – The Colonel* stands up to that innovation with full-bodied character and deep earthy tones. For a spicier twist, the *Alec Bradley Black Market Estelí* introduces dark pepper and leather—ideal for adventurous palates seeking layered intensity.

## 27. J.W. Kelly & Co. (Chattanooga) – *Tennessee Whiskey*

With roots in post–Civil War Tennessee, J.W. Kelly honors its legacy as both a distiller and tobacconist—making it a natural fit for pairing. The brand's Reserve Straight Bourbon, known for its notes of caramel, dried fruit, and toasted spice, finds a bold partner in *Antebellum No. 1 – The Colonel.* This cigar's rich cocoa and earthy depth complement the bourbon's complexity. For a deeply symbolic pairing, consider *Exsul*—a Dominican puro of Cuban-seed origin, rolled in the traditional *entubado* method and built on the philosophy of exile and resilience. Its rich, structured draw reflects J.W. Kelly's own revivalist spirit and tobacco heritage. Together, they form a tribute to memory, refinement, and enduring craft. And finally, for a more traditional match, try a *Perdomo Reserve 10th Anniversary Maduro*, whose creamy finish and dark chocolate notes echo the bourbon's layered warmth.

## 28. Old Dominick Distillery (Memphis) – *Tennessee Whiskey*

Old Dominick's flagship bourbon leans toward a bolder, oak-forward profile with underlying spice and dried fruit. *Exsul*—a Dominican puro made entirely from Cuban-seed tobaccos and rolled in the traditional *entubado* style—makes an exceptional match. Its layered complexity, with notes of dark cocoa, fig, and slow-burning spice, mirrors the whiskey's structure and richness while adding a quiet elegance to the pairing. For a contrasting modern twist, the *E.P.*

*Carrillo Dusk* offers a creamier draw with espresso and wood tones, creating a richly layered finish with broader aromatic reach.

## 29. Sugarlands Distilling Co. (Gatlinburg) – *Tennessee Whiskey*

Better known for its moonshine, Sugarlands' Roaming Man Tennessee Straight Rye Whiskey adds rye spice and sweetness to a softer profile. That makes them a great match for *Antebellum No. 2 – The Statesman*, whose light wood, creamy texture, and subtle sweetness echo and elevate the gentler notes. Alternatively, try the *Arturo Fuente Hemingway Short Story*—a compact, flavorful cigar that balances nuance and nostalgia.

## 30. Leiper's Fork Distillery (Franklin) – *Tennessee Whiskey*

This craft distillery focuses on heritage techniques and small-batch expressions that often feature a mellow spice and deep oak character. *Antebellum No. 1 – The Colonel* mirrors this depth with full-bodied richness and historical resonance. For a boutique complement, consider the *La Aroma de Cuba Mi Amor*, whose cocoa, earth, and pepper notes echo the bourbon's warm finish and honor tradition with flair.

# Bibliography

**Chapter 1: Origins of an American Pairing (1600s–1800s)**

- Carp, Benjamin L. *Rebels Rising: Cities and the American Revolution*. Oxford University Press, 2007.

- Crowgey, Henry G. *Kentucky Bourbon: The Early Years of Whiskeymaking*. University Press of Kentucky, 2013.

- Goodman, Jordan. *Tobacco in History: The Cultures of Dependence*. Routledge, 1993.

- Kwass, Michael. *The Consumer Revolution, 1650-1800*. Cambridge University Press, 2022.

- Rainford, Tyler. "Distilled Spirits, the Self, and Society in Early Modern England (1660–1760)." *PhD diss.*, University of Bristol, 2024.

- Raitz, Karl. *Making Bourbon: A Geographical History of Distilling in Nineteenth-Century Kentucky*. University Press of Kentucky, 2020.

- Riley, Edward M. "The Town Acts of Colonial Virginia." *The Journal of Southern History* 16, no. 3 (1950): 306-323.

- Rooney, John F., and Paul L. Butt. "Beer, Bourbon and Boone's Farm: A Geographical Examination of Alcoholic Drink in the United States." *Journal of Popular Culture* 12, no. 3 (1978): 411-427.

- Scribner, Vaughn P. "Imperial Pubs: British American Taverns as Spaces of Empire, 1700-1783." *PhD diss.*, University of Kansas, 2013.

- Surface, George T. "Geographic Influence on the Economic History of Virginia." *Bulletin of the American Geographical Society* 39, no. 7 (1907): 397-409.

- Thompson, Peter. *Rum Punch & Revolution: Taverngoing & Public Life in Eighteenth Century Philadelphia*. University of Pennsylvania Press, 1999.

- Veach, Michael R. *Kentucky Bourbon Whiskey: An American Heritage*. University Press of Kentucky, 2013.

- Wertenbaker, Thomas J. *The Planters of Colonial Virginia*. Princeton University Press, 1959.

## Chapter 2: The Golden Age

- Cooper, Patricia A. *Once a Cigar Maker: Men, Women, and Work Culture in American Cigar Factories, 1900-1919*. University of Illinois Press, 1987.

- Felten, Eric. *How's Your Drink?: Cocktails, Culture, and the Art of Drinking Well*. Agate Surrey, 2009.

- Holt, Michael F. *The Rise and Fall of the American Whig Party: Jacksonian Politics and the Onset of the Civil War*. Oxford University Press, 1999.

- Howlett, Leon. *The Kentucky Bourbon Experience: A Visual Tour of Kentucky's Bourbon Distilleries*. Acclaim Press, 2012.

- Mitenbuler, Reid. *Bourbon Empire: The Past and Future of America's Whiskey*. Viking, 2015.

- Perelman, Richard B. *Perelman's Pocket Cyclopedia of Havana Cigars*. Perelman, Pioneer & Co., 2006.

- Smith, Andrew F. *Drinking History: Fifteen Turning Points in the Making of American Beverages*. Columbia University Press, 2013.

- Watts, Steven. *The People's Tycoon: Henry Ford and the American Century*. Alfred A. Knopf, 2005.

## Chapter 3: Prohibition & the Post-War Decline (1920s-1960s)

- Burnham, John C. *Bad Habits: Drinking, Smoking, Taking Drugs, Gambling, Sexual Misbehavior, and Swearing in American History*. New York University Press, 1993.

- Courtwright, David T. *Forces of Habit: Drugs and the Making of the Modern World*. Harvard University Press, 2001.

- Lender, Mark Edward, and James Kirby Martin. *Drinking in America: A History*. The Free Press, 1982.

- Okrent, Daniel. *Last Call: The Rise and Fall of Prohibition*. Scribner, 2010.

- Rorabaugh, W. J. *Prohibition: A Concise History*. Oxford University Press, 2018.

## Chapter 4: The Cuban Embargo & Industry Reinvention (1962-1990s)

- Babun, Teo A., and Victor Andres Triay. *The Cuban Revolution: Years of Promise*. University Press of Florida, 2005.

- *Cigar Aficionado*. New York: M. Shanken Communications, various issues, 1992–1999.
- Cowdery, Charles K. *Bourbon, Straight: The Uncut and Unfiltered Story of American Whiskey*. Made and Bottled in Kentucky, 2004.
- Font, Mauricio A., and Alfonso W. Quiroz, eds. *The Cuban Republic and José Martí: Reception and Use of a National Symbol*. Lexington Books, 2006.
- Huckelbridge, Dane. *Bourbon: A History of the American Spirit*. New York: William Morrow, 2014.
- Minnick, Fred. *Bourbon Curious: A Simple Tasting Guide for the Savvy Drinker*. Zenith Press, 2014.
- Mitenbuler, Reid. *Bourbon Empire: The Past and Future of America's Whiskey*. Viking, 2015.
- Sweig, Julia. *Inside the Cuban Revolution: Fidel Castro and the Urban Underground*. Harvard University Press, 2002.
- Tilley, Nannie M. *The Bright-Tobacco Industry, 1860-1929*. University of North Carolina Press, 1948.
- Veach, Michael R. *Kentucky Bourbon Whiskey: An American Heritage*. University Press of Kentucky, 2013.
- Wallach, Jennifer Jensen. *How America Eats: A Social History of U.S. Food and Culture*. Rowman & Littlefield, 2013.

## Chapter 5: The Renaissance

- Cowdery, Charles K. *Bourbon, Straight: The Uncut and Unfiltered Story of American Whiskey*. Made and Bottled in Kentucky, 2004.
- Minnick, Fred. *Bourbon: The Rise, Fall, and Rebirth of an American Whiskey*. Voyageur Press, 2016.
- Veach, Michael R. *Kentucky Bourbon Whiskey: An American Heritage*. University Press of Kentucky, 2013.

## Chapter 6: The Sensory Connection

*Bourbon and Whisky Chemistry*

- Mosedale, J. R., and Jean-Louis Puech. "Wood Maturation of Distilled Beverages." *Trends in Food Science & Technology* 9, no. 3 (1998): 95–101.

*Tobacco and Cigar Chemistry*

- Davis, Daniel L., and Mark T. Nielsen, eds. *Tobacco: Production, Chemistry and Technology.* Blackwell Science, 1999.

*Olfaction, Flavor Perception, and Retronasal Smell*

- Rozin, Paul. "'Taste-Smell Confusions' and the Duality of the Olfactory Sense." *Perception & Psychophysics* 31, no. 4 (1982): 397–401.
- Shepherd, Gordon M. *Neurogastronomy: How the Brain Creates Flavor and Why It Matters.* Columbia University Press, 2012.
- Small, Dana M., and John Prescott. "Odor/Taste Integration and the Perception of Flavor." *Experimental Brain Research* 166, nos. 3–4 (2005): 345–357.

## Chapter 7: Molecular Flavor Interactions

*Phenolic Compounds, Terpenes, and Esters*

- Polášková, Pavla, Julian Herszage, and Susan E. Ebeler. "Wine Flavor: Chemistry in a Glass." *Chemical Society Reviews* 37, no. 11 (2008): 2478–2489.

*Whisky and Spirits Flavor Chemistry*

- Piggott, J. R., R. Sharp, and R. E. B. Duncan, eds., *The Science and Technology of Whiskies.* Longman Scientific & Technical, 1989.
- Russell, Inge, and Graham Stewart, eds. *Whisky: Technology, Production and Marketing.* 2nd ed. Academic Press, 2014.
- Lee, K.-Y. Monica, Alistair Paterson, John R. Piggott, and Graeme D. Richardson. "Origins of Flavour in Whiskies and a Revised Flavour Wheel: A Review." *Journal of the Institute of Brewing* 107, no. 5 (2001): 287–313.

*Olfaction, Cross-Modal Perception, and Flavor Neuroscience*

- Shepherd, Gordon M. *Neurogastronomy: How the Brain Creates Flavor and Why It Matters.* New York: Columbia University Press, 2012.
- Stevenson, Richard J. *The Psychology of Flavour.* Oxford: Oxford University Press, 2009.
- Spence, Charles. *Gastrophysics: The New Science of Eating.* New York: Viking, 2017.

*Ethanol's Role in Flavor Release and Perception*

- Robinson, Anthony L., Susan E. Ebeler, Hildegarde Heymann, Peter K. Boss, Paul S. Solomon, and Robert D. Trengove. "Interactions between Wine

Volatile Compounds and Grape and Wine Matrix Components Influence Aroma Compound Headspace Partitioning." *Journal of Agricultural and Food Chemistry* 57, no. 21 (2009): 10313–10322.

### Chapter 8: Regional Terroir – Geography's Flavor Fingerprint

- Broom, Dave. *Whiskey: The Definitive World Guide*. DK Publishing, 2017.
- Curtis, Wayne. *And a Bottle of Rum: A History of the New World in Ten Cocktails*. Crown, 2018.
- Pérez, Louis A., Jr. *Cuba: Between Reform and Revolution*. Oxford University Press, 2015.
- Raitz, Karl. *Making Bourbon: A Geographical History of Distilling in Nineteenth-Century Kentucky*. University Press of Kentucky, 2020.
- Stubbs, Jean. *Tobacco on the Periphery: A Case Study in Cuban Labour History, 1860–1958*. Cambridge University Press, 1985.

### Chapter 9: Understanding Bourbon Profiles & Pairing Strategies

- Broom, Dave. *The World Atlas of Whisky: More Than 200 Distilleries Explored and 750 Expressions Tasted*. 2nd ed. Mitchell Beazley, 2014.
- Bryson, Lew. *Tasting Whiskey: An Insider's Guide to the Unique Pleasures of the World's Finest Spirits*. Storey Publishing, 2014.
- McGee, Harold. *On Food and Cooking: The Science and Lore of the Kitchen*. New York: Scribner, 2004.
- Risen, Clay. *Bourbon: The Story of Kentucky Whiskey*. Ten Speed Press, 2021.

### Chapter 10: The Art of Tasting & Pairing Like a Pro

- Bryson, Lew. *Tasting Whiskey: An Insider's Guide to the Unique Pleasures of the World's Finest Spirits*. Storey Publishing, 2014.
- McGee, Harold. *On Food and Cooking: The Science and Lore of the Kitchen*. Rev. ed. Scribner, 2004.
- Minnick, Fred. *Bourbon Curious: A Tasting Guide for the Savvy Drinker*. Voyageur Press, 2015.
- Spence, Charles. *Gastrophysics: The New Science of Eating*. Viking, 2017.
- Shepherd, Gordon M. *Neurogastronomy: How the Brain Creates Flavor and Why It Matters*. Columbia University Press, 2012.

# Index

**L**

- Limestone water
  - impact on bourbon, 37–39
  - regional significance, 138–140
- Leiper's Fork Distillery, 191
- Lux Row (distillery), 186

**M**

- Macanudo (cigar brand), 74, 102
- Maker's Mark (distillery), 44, 97, 183
- Michter's Fort Nelson (distillery), 187
- Molecular flavor interactions, 127–130
- Mouthfeel in pairing, 118–121

**N**

- Neuroscience of taste, 129–132
- Nelson's Green Brier (distillery), 189
- New Orleans
  - cultural confluence, 57–59

**O**

- Oak barrels
  - aging process, 113–116
  - flavor contribution, 113–116
- Old Dominick Distillery, 190
- Old Forester (distillery), 186
- Oliva (cigar brand), 184, 185, 186, 188

**P**

- Padrón (cigar brand), 183, 184, 186, 188
- Pairing strategies
  - enhancing experience, 151–157
  - practical tips, 156–157
- Pop culture's role in renaissance, 98–99
- Post-war decline (1920s–1960s), 67–77

## V

- Van Winkle (bourbon family), 95–96, 98, 102–103, 106, 109, 115, 156, 174
- Vanilla notes, 113–116, 130, 133–144, 162–167
- Vanillin, 112, 116, 129

## W

- Water, limestone-filtered, 37–39, 138–140
- Wild Turkey (distillery), 44, 136, 185
- Wilderness Trail (distillery), 188
- Willett (distillery), 186
- Whiskey styles, American vs Scotch, 75, 97, 104
- Wheated bourbons, 149–151
- Wood influence on bourbon, 113–116
- Woodford Reserve (distillery), 184

# About the Author

**Sebastian Saviano** is a writer and researcher whose work explores American craft, ritual, and identity. He is the author of *America's Cigar Story: The History, Politics, and Legacy of Cigars from 1762 to the Modern Era*, the first volume of *The American Cigar Series*. *Smoke & Oak* is the second.

Trained in political theory at Georgetown University, he writes about the cultural lives of the things Americans make, drink, and pass around the table — and what those things have to say about who we are.

# About *The American Cigar Series*

**Volume I — *America's Cigar Story: The History, Politics, and Legacy of Cigars from 1762 to the Modern Era***
The foundational volume of the series. From colonial Virginia tobacco fields through Civil War generals, postwar prosperity, and the boutique revival, *America's Cigar Story* traces how a hand-rolled product became a fixture of American economic, political, and cultural life.

**Volume II — *Smoke & Oak: The Shared Legacy of Bourbon and Cigars***
*(this volume)*

**Volume III — *The American Puro: The All-American Cigar's Forgotten History***
*(forthcoming)* The story of cigars made entirely from U.S.-grown tobacco — a tradition older than most readers realize, and one being quietly revived by a new generation of American growers and rollers.

**Volume IV — *Cigar America: Tobacco, Masculinity, and the Myth of Power***
*(forthcoming)* A cultural essay on how the cigar became shorthand for power, defiance, and American masculinity — from Grant's stogie to Castro's Cohiba, from boardroom rituals to Tony Montana's final scene. What remains, the book asks, when the smoke clears?

www.ingramcontent.com/pod-product-compliance
Lightning Source LLC
Chambersburg PA
CBHW051618120626
46551CB00014B/1845

* 9 7 9 8 9 9 8 5 1 1 7 6 9 *